# Corporate Environmental Policy And Government Regulation

**MONOGRAPHS IN ORGANIZATIONAL
BEHAVIOR AND INDUSTRIAL RELATIONS, VOLUME 17**

*Editor:*  Samuel B. Bacharach, Department of Organizational Behavior, New
York State School of Industrial and Labor Relations, Cornell
University

# MONOGRAPHS IN ORGANIZATIONAL BEHAVIOR AND INDUSTRIAL RELATIONS

Edited by
## Samuel B. Bacharach
*Department of Organizational Behavior*
*New York State School of Industrial and Labor Relations*
*Cornell University*

# Corporate Environmental Policy and Government Regulation

by **L.R. JONES**

*Naval Postgraduate School*

**JOHN H. BALDWIN**

*University of Oregon*

 **JAI PRESS INC.**

*Greenwich, Connecticut*          *London, England*

*658.408*
*J77c*

**Library of Congress Cataloging-in-Publication Data**

Corporate environmental policy and government regulation / edited by
  L.R. Jones, John H. Baldwin.
      p.      cm. — (Monographs in organizational behavior and
  industrial relations ; v. 17)
    Includes bibliographical references and index.
    ISBN 1-55938-759-9
    1. Industrial management—Environmental aspects.   2. Environmental
  policy.   3. Environmental law.   4. Social responsibility of
  business.      I. Jones, L. R.   II. Baldwin, John H.   II. Series.
  HD69.P6C668   1994
  658.4'08—dc20                                                        94-14651
                                                                          CIP

*Copyright © 1994 JAI Press Inc.*
*55 Old Post Road No. 2*
*Greenwich, Connecticut 06830*

*JAI Press Ltd.*
*The Courtyard*
*28 High Street*
*Hampton Hill*
*Middlesex TW12 1PD*
*England*

*ISBN: 1-55938-759-9*

*Library of Congress Catalog Number: 94-14651*

*Manufactured in the United States of America*

# Contents

# List of Tables

# Acknowledgments

A considerable amount of work goes into the research and preparation of any manuscript for publication. In the case of this manuscript the authors received assistance from a variety of sources. Part of the research for this book was conducted by L. R. Jones as a J. William Fulbright Scholar under the auspices of the Council for the International Exchange of Scholars. Funding for research was provided by the Kraft General Foods Corporation. Thanks as well is given to the U.S. Navy for providing additional research support and sponsorship. Appreciation also is owed to Dr. Norman London and the Academic Relations Division, Canadian Embassy and the Department of Foreign Affairs and International Trade Government of Canada for funding some of the research that produced this book.

This research could not have been completed without the assistance of a number of corporate environmental affairs officers and staff, and the staff of state, provincial, and federal government regulatory agencies in the United States and Canada. In particular, assistance and data were provided by the U.S. Environmental Protection Agency and Environmental Canada. Additional materials and assistance were obtained from the Environmental Policy Center, and the Environmental Law Institute. The U.S. Business Roundtable also contributed valuable data for analysis. Other data on corporate and government environmental policy in Canada were provided by the Canadian Federal Environmental Assessment Review Office, Industry, Science and Technology Canada, the British Columbia

Commission on Resources and Environment, and the British Columbia Business Round Table. Finally, several colleagues contributed research effort and writing to this book. Jennifer Snyder contributed to Chapter 2, Frank Priznar wrote the first draft to Chapter 4, and Fred Thompson contributed to Chapters 5 and 6. While their contributions and those of the sponsors noted above are appreciated, responsibility for the contents of this book is solely that of the authors.

The authors wish to dedicate this book to corporate environmental affairs officers whose efforts to persuade their firms to be more responsive in establishing and meeting public demand for environmental protection and preservation often go unnoticed and unappreciated.

# Part I

**CORPORATE
ENVIRONMENTALISM**

# Chapter I

# *Corporate Environmental Policy:*
# *A Framework for Analysis*

## INTRODUCTION

To determine the prospective role of regulation, self-regulation, ethics, morality, and other factors in producing responsible behavior with respect to the environment it is necessary to inquire whether regulation or other approaches are most effective in achieving what is deemed to be socially desirable behavior. This perspective suggests the question: Under what circumstances will a regulatory approach versus self-regulation and other incentives achieve publicly desirable ends? An interesting test of this question may be found in government efforts to enforce environmental policy and law to modify the behavior of polluting firms in the private sector. This book explores the incentives that appear to influence corporations to adapt socially responsible environmental policy. In particular, it attempts to assess the role of eight factors in promoting corporate environmentalism: increasing costs related to environmental protection and compliance, consumer demand and market competition, environmental interest group pressure, government regulation, action and rulings by courts in support of environmental laws and challenges, ethics or morality, public opinion, and media attention.

# THE CONTENT FOR CORPORATE ENVIRONMENTAL ACTION

Corporate environmentalism appears to have come of age. There is no doubt that corporate executives, boards of directors, and stockholders are rapidly becoming aware of the importance of environmental policy and planning as a component of business strategy and marketing in the 1990s. Corporate boardrooms are filled with discussion of how to respond to consumer preferences for "green" products and services, how to placate or satisfy environmental interest groups, and how to manage interaction with government regulatory agencies. Corporations are hiring environmental affairs officers and vice presidents for environmental programs and are providing them with staffs to develop environmental plans and policies. New board members and committees have been added to corporate directorates to represent environmental interest group concerns. Environmental lawyers serve on retainer to corporate legal counsels. Consultants are hired to advise corporations on environmental planning, marketing, advertising, recycling, waste disposal, and are performing environmental audits at record pace (Industry and Environment, 1988). Television, radio, and the print media are covered with ads that attempt to appeal to emergent green consumer demand. Allegations of "green fraud" are made by government regulators and environmental interest group representatives over false advertising and product labeling.

Amid all this activity several crucial questions must be addressed: Is any of this activity different from other fads that have caused corporations to invest in new marketing strategies? Do corporations operate in a more environmentally safe or benign manner now than they did before the second coming of the environmental movement that has been carried along by baby-boomer consumer power? Is there an emergence of a new set of corporate ethics? Are businesses cooperating more with governmental regulatory agencies now than in the past? Is the Earth any better off for all of this action or are we witnessing only a slowing of the pace of degradation?

There are no easy means for answering these questions in a comprehensive manner. As is the case in evaluation of any socioeconomic trend, there are signs of hope for the new environmentalism in the corporate setting, and there are clear signals of failure and alarm. To say that there is an increasing environmental awareness among consumers and corporate executives is not to say that this concern has been effectively translated into action to make the air and water cleaner, to reduce the production of hazardous and toxic wastes, to increase conservation, recycling and energy efficiency, or to have any impact on the staggering problem of waste disposal in a wasteful and packaging-crazed world. Nor can we observe with any certainty that progress made in the United States or elsewhere is sufficient to offset the increase in environmental problems in developing nations, the atmosphere or anywhere else in the world (Ridgeway, 1970; Hardin and Baden, 1977; Plumwood and Routley, 1982). Part of the environmental concept is "one world," that is, that there is in essence an existential reality about environmental degradation (Cohen, 1983; Anderson, 1987; Abram, 1988; Greenpeace Chronicles, 1988). Whatever happens from Brazil or Eastern Europe, Russia, China, or Malaysia, or from pole to pole will eventually affect everyone on the planet (Balfour, 1944; Carson, 1961; Carson, 1962; Bergon, 1980; Fox, 1981; Frey, 1983; Warwick, 1984; Arnold, 1987; Bahro, 1986a/b; Caplan, 1990; Carmody, 1990). The issue is not whether effects will spread but how and when. Deterioration of the earth's ozone layer, the spread of radiation from nuclear power plant disasters, the sweeping destruction of the world's forest resources, the potential outcome of the greenhouse effect and global warming—all of these events serve to remind us that, whether we like it or not, we all are environmentalists in that we must try to survive and remain healthy on this planet (Collingwood, 1945; Pinchot, 1947; Pinchot, 1967; Henderson, 1981; Commoner, 1990; Greg and Posner, 1990; Heritage Forests Society, 1990).

Part of the question posed in this study is whether corporations are "part of the problem or part of the solution." The obvious answer is that they are both. Still, it is somewhat revolutionary to think of corporations, typically vilified by environmentalists as the creators of many if not most environmental problems, as part of the solution. Rather, traditionally it has been the environmental activist or government regulator who has been characterized as the savior of the environment working to thwart the greedy scions of industrial wealth (Porritt, 1985; Bennet and Di Lorenzo, 1985;

Foreman, 1986, 1987; Cohn, 1987; Watson, 1990). However, in the 1990s the reality has dawned that, in fact, it is the wealth of corporations that must be combined with the money of taxpayers and private philanthropists to invest in environmental mitigation, clean-up, and protection measures. There is no avoiding the reality that corporations need to be a part of the grand strategy of environmental action in this decade and the century to come (Croner, 1983; Capra and Spretnak, 1984; Pezzey, 1988; Collison, 1989; Swolop and Barrett, 1990; Weiner, 1990).

## FRAMEWORK FOR ANALYSIS OF CORPORATE ENVIRONMENTALISM

A framework of causal factors provides the basis for development of a methodological design to study corporate environmentalism. From the perspective of experimental design, corporate policy, and management response to environmental problems and issues comprises the dependent variable. The independent variables are the actions, events, and values that influence corporate policy development and implementation. For purposes of analysis it may be hypothesized that corporate environmental policy and management is driven by at least eight variables. These variables are not listed in any particular order given that data have been assessed empirically to substantiate the relationships:

1. increasing costs related to the environment,
2. consumer demand and market competition,
3. environmental interest group pressure,
4. government regulation and enforcement practices,
5. actions and rulings by courts in support of environmental laws and challenges,
6. public opinion,
7. news media attention to corporate environmental problems,
8. culturally-based ethnic norms and perceptions of moral behavior.

Each of these variables may be examined quantitatively and qualitatively to determine the strength of their influence on the dependent variable. Other independent variables may be identified and tested. The primary hypothesis to be tested in this book is that these variables have influenced and will continue to influence the development and implementation of socially responsible corporate environmental policy. The null-hypothesis is that these variables have not and will not influence corporate policy and management. The results of this analysis would permit the formulation of a theoretical model to explain corporate environmental policymaking. This model would depict the strength and relationships between variables. The model might then be applied to guide private and public sector policy formulation and management decision making. This book makes an initial attempt to describe the dynamics of how these variables appear to have influenced corporate environmental policy. The variables hypothesized to influence corporate environmentalism are examined below.

## COSTS OF ENVIRONMENTAL PROTECTION AND LEGAL COMPLIANCE

Corporations small and large face increasing costs for management of liquid and solid wastes, hazardous and toxic materials, and other by-products of production. The costs of waste storage and disposal have increased dramatically in many areas of North America and the world, and they are projected to increase further unless breakthroughs in recycling and storage and disposal technology are implemented. Further, energy costs also have increased and will continue to do so in most nations until conservation and technological advances are found to cap their growth. Thus, corporations are driven to pursue recycling programs, improved waste management methodologies and energy conservation as a means for containing growth in production costs. Many corporations have discovered that, in fact, they can achieve considerable savings through increased efficiency in waste management and energy conservation. Investment in waste and heat recycling, for example, has proven cost-effective in numerous settings. In addition, corporations find compliance with environmental laws and regulation to be costly, but they are driven to comply to avoid legal liability, related potential losses resulting from lawsuits, and fines or other penalties.

However, there is another side to this issue. In many instances corporations have chosen to relocate production facilities to take advantage of lower waste disposal and/or energy costs. This strategy may prove successful in the short run, but it may also indicate that business is simply attempting to shift the burden of disposal and energy production into another jurisdiction. This is not a problem for the corporation until the advantage of relocation disappears. However, from the standpoint of public policy, such strategies may cause more problems than they resolve.

## CONSUMER DEMAND IN THE MARKET

A second factor that appears to be stimulating corporate environmentalism is consumer demand and market competition (Fisher, 1989; Tokar, 1990). As consumer-environmentalists have gained income they have increased their power to influence corporate policy directly through the marketplace (Pollution Probe, 1990). The demand for "green" products has increased dramatically over the past few years, leading to some debate over the exact nature of the definition of such products. Corporations appear to have responded initially to the "green" demand with a wave of product advertising and packaging changes. The first response was simply to stress the environmentally benign or safe and desirable nature of the product as it existed without any or significant modification. Thus, where packaging was made of partially recycled paper, for example, this fact was placed prominently onto the packaging of the product and mentioned in advertising. This type of cosmetic change apparently produced a highly favorable initial response from some consumer segments. However, there have been some serious questions raised by the Federal Trade Commission and consumer activists about the validity of many claims made by manufacturers about the environmentally benign or safe and desirable characteristics of products shown on packaging. In the United States and Canada, some producers have been ordered by government regulators to remove statements from packaging because they could mislead consumers about the true nature of the product or its production process.

The second phase of corporate responsiveness to green consumerism seems to have involved evaluation of the nature of products and production processes to determine what changes could be made in product design and production to, in fact, improve environmental performance beyond mere advertising and labeling. This phase of response has resulted in the modification of production to reduce production of pollutants, to increase recycling of materials and recycling of products and packaging, plus evaluation of natural resource consumption in production (e.g., water), as well as greater attention to energy efficiency among selected firms. The third phase of response to environmental consumerism taken by selected corporations has involved the partial or complete redesign of products and production processes to achieve environmental objectives.

## INTEREST GROUP PRESSURE

A third factor that appears to have influenced corporate environmental policy formation is public interest group pressure on business and industry to mitigate the environmental consequences of production and consumption. Public interest groups have become increasingly effective in influencing corporate policy and performance by use of the courts, the media, and government legislative and regulatory agency agendas (Arnold, 1982; Papadikis, 1984; Pepper, 1985; Foreman, 1986; Foreman, 1987; Cohen, 1988; Greenpeace, 1990; Phillips, 1990). As the ability of interest groups to communicate among themselves and with the public through the media has increased, the leverage brought to bear by such action has produced real results (Steger and Bowenmaster, 1990; Watson, 1990). Part of the change described above in corporate policy is in direct response to interest group pressure.

Increased sophistication on the part of consumer and interest group lobbyists and legal representatives has forced some firms and persuaded others to evaluate the environmental component of product management and corporate policy, and in some instances to place members of interest groups onto their boards of directors. Many corporations also have formed committees of their boards to assist in formulating environmental policy and plans, and to deal with interest group demands. The extent of interest group activity and some of the strategies and tactics used to influence corporate policy has been the subject of considerable research interest and media reporting (Watson and Rogers, 1982; Poritt, 1985; Weston, 1986; Tuer, 1990; Watson, 1990).

## GOVERNMENT ENVIRONMENTAL REGULATION

A fourth component driving the new environmentalism in corporations is government regulatory pressure brought about through passage of environmental laws and adoption of administrative rules to force business and industry to comply with standards of performance, compliance, and behavior (Pepper, 1985; Hays, 1987). As a result of public demand and interest group pressure, elected officials have responded with a wide array of laws to force environmental compliance on the private sector (Thompson and Jones, 1982). While major environmental policy acts have gained the most attention from the public and the media, the preponderance of regulation results from administrative rules developed by regulatory agencies in the executive branch of government at deferral, state/provincial, and local levels. The extent of regulatory overlap between jurisdictions is an issue of concern for business and public agencies attempting to enforce the laws. Because the force of law is initially established in statute and then interpreted administratively, the number of participants involved in implementing legislation is large, and the degree of discretion afforded regulatory agencies is often quite broad. This also presents additional complexity to firms attempting to comply fully with the law.

An additional factor relating to enforcement is the use of fines and penalties to force compliance. In theory, unless a fine is equal to the cost of compliance there is a financial incentive for business to simply ignore the law and pay fines. Other variables enter the calculus of compliance including the probability of getting caught and frequency of violations and fines. However, it has taken more than a decade for government regulatory agencies and the elected officials that budget them to adopt what is termed a market-based approach to enforcement supported by economists rather than the command-control (you must do this/must not do that) regulatory method preferred from a purely legalistic view of enforcement. While the market-based approach including the sale of rights to pollute to a specific level (marketable ' rights) is generally objectionable to environmentalists, it is often the only feasible, cost-effective option to permit compromise between government rules and the economic and employment demands of industry (Pezzey, 1988; Conway, 1990).

Businesses have also shown a greater willingness to comply with regulation where regulatory agencies do not attempt to enforce one best technology, but instead allow the private sector to seek compliance against a set of performance targets using methods of their own design and fitting their own circumstance and financial investment strategy. More cooperation between business and government has produced a new era of compliance for selected firms and components of industries (Canadian Manufacturing Association, 1990). However, there is still much progress to be made in achieving compliance with environmental laws already on the books but not enforced. From the government perspective, the budget is a key constraint to enforcement effectiveness. From the business view, the answer to compliance lies in more reasonable laws and more market-based approaches to enforcement. Also, in an international context, the degree of compatibility or conflict between the laws of different nations is an important factor influencing industrial and labor policy towards the environment, as well as government regulatory strategy.

## JUDICIAL RULINGS AND ACTIONS

A fifth factor that seems to have brought about increased corporate environmental awareness is action by courts of law in support of challenges to the actions of business and industry (Sutherland and Parker, 1988; Turner, 1988). In fact, use of the courts has become a refined tactic by environmental interest groups, and corporations themselves have learned a great deal from their strategies (Canan and Pring, 1985). While the courts have become inextricably entwined in the relationship between business, interest groups, and government, they attempt to be impartial regarding the placement of blame for environmental error, attempting to rule instead on the basis of case law and interpretation of the intent of the law and of those accused of violating environmental laws and rules. However, given the progressive nature of environmental law over the past several decades and the activism of environmental law specialists, business leaders often have perceived the courts as tools of interest groups, and unduly influenced by the media. In turn, environmental interest groups have viewed the courts as the last stopgap against development of natural resources or industrial pollution production and distribution.

The trend in the law has been to increase the volume of statute substantially, which has placed an enormous burden for interpretation and adjudication on the courts. The trends that have emerged as a consequence are; (a) an increase in the cost of litigation to all parties—business, government, and interest groups, and (b) attempts to resolve disputes by means other than the courts. Nonjudicial dispute resolution may become the preferred approach, where possible and practical, for business and for interest groups and government to negotiate resolution to seemingly intractable disagreements (Pat-Delbridge Associates, 1990). This is the case primarily because use of the courts is very costly, seldom produces a quick outcome, and is almost always subject to appeal. Nonjudicial dispute resolution may be less costly and produce better results for all parties in some circumstances. Although the extent of the use of the courts in many nations is not nearly as great as in the United States, nonjudicial dispute resolution appears to be on the rise internationally.

## PUBLIC OPINION

An additional factor that clearly appears to influence corporate environmentalism is public opinion and related media attention to it. Public opinion surveys in Canada, the United States, and elsewhere in the world indicate a high public concern for environmental protection and preservation (Cotgrove and Duff, 1981; Anglemeyer and Seagraves, 1984; Anderson, 1991). Public opinion on environmental issues can have a profound impact on government regulation of business, particularly when reported in the news media. In turn, public opinion may be influenced by media coverage of environmental issues and problems including disasters, for example, a nuclear power plant failure or toxic waste spills (Whelan, 1985; Gibson, 1990). However, it is not clear how long media attention to a particular event lasts in terms of its effect on public opinion. Still, elected officials may be influenced by public opinion and media attention to events and issues so that they pass laws that stiffen and broaden government regulation significantly. Special interest pressure by environmental lobby groups may hasten government action if it is timed properly. In responding, elected officials may enhance their opportunity for reelection. Any response to a major environmental problem that receives media attention is likely to be viewed favorably by elected officials as well as government regulators. Legislation passed to respond to specific problems inevitably affects business and the economy.

A variable that seems to affect public opinion on the need for action on environmental issues is the health or robustness of the economy. During periods of recession and slow or no GNP growth, public priorities seem to shift away from environmental problems. Conversely, in a growing economy where wealth is increasing, the public seems to place a higher priority on environmental protection. However, other factors intervene to complicate the assessment of public opinion on the need for environmental protection. For example, one variable that may influence public opinion is the level of taxation or tax effort required in a jurisdiction. Tax effort is measured by tax level relative to the wealth of the tax base, that is, how much wealth or income is available to be taxed and how heavily it is taxed. Higher taxes and tax effort may depress public opinion on demand for environmental protection.

## NEWS MEDIA ATTENTION
## TO CORPORATE ENVIRONMENTAL PROBLEMS

The news media appear to play a role in influencing corporate environmentalism by reporting environmental problems and public attitudes on the need for solutions to these problems. Interest groups have become effective in using the media (or being used by the media) to focus public attention on environmental issues. The media as an industry has an incentive to report environmental problems when it is perceived that such reporting will interest readers, listeners, and viewers in that increased demand for such information may be translated into advertising revenues. However, part of the explanation for media attention to environmental issues also may be explained by editorial or management policy based on ethics, that is, that reporting problems will lead to solutions in the public interest. However, in some instances media reporting may distort public perceptions of hazards and risks and over-stimulate demand on government to solve problems in ways that are not cost beneficial (Beckmann, 1973; Gibson, 1990; Thompson and Jones, 1982).

It may be argued that in some instances media attention has stimulated public ire to the extent that elected officials have been pressured to take action immediately without thorough understanding of the nature of the problem, alternative solutions, and costs related to alternatives. The media may point out correctly that such judgments are not for them to make and the legitimate role of government is to determine the best course of action to respond to public demand. However, the tradition of investigative reporting suggests that many members of the news media believe that they should play a strong role in influencing public, government, and corporate action.

## CULTURALLY BASED ETHICAL NORMS AND PERCEPTIONS OF MORAL BEHAVIOR

An eighth factor that appears to have contributed to corporate environmental concern is morality based, which in turn rests on cognitive perceptions of right and wrong (Fiskin, 1984). Threat perception and relative degree of acceptable risk may be viewed to influence ethical behavior (Gunn, 1980; Attfield, 1983; Van Den Bosch, 1983; Hanson, 1986; Callicot, 1989; Daly and Cobb, 1989). Also, a key variable stimulating this new environmental morality may be the efficiency of communications systems. Unless an issue or risk is communicated it does not affect perception of risk and ethical behavior. If it is accepted that there are real differences between individual and group perceptions of right and wrong, and that perceptions are affected by specific circumstance, then it follows that perceptions of ethical or unethical behavior, risk and acceptable levels of environmental purity or degradation will vary across populations and events. These variations ensure ethical disputes over corporate and government environmental policy and practice.

The extent to which environmental degradation results in risk to health is certainly a matter for scientific exploration. However, the results of tests often are inconclusive (Thompson and Jones, 1982). The determination of dose-response relationships across heterogeneous populations with different levels of exposure and varying genetic and behavioral adaptability severely complicates the regulatory task. From the perception of business, government has been too willing to legislate and enforce environmental laws before sufficient evidence is present to support the need for control. This has driven the costs of compliance far above what is necessary from the view of industry. However, the perception of environmental interest groups is that the ethical burden of proof for safety and health lies with business, and that the role of government is, therefore, to err on the conservative side of risk exposure, regardless of the real and opportunity costs of this policy stance.

While it may not always be expected that science or the courts will enforce ethical and moral precepts, it is possible to trace part of the origins of the new environmentalism in corporations to a desire to be perceived as "good citizens," acting responsibly in a community where many values relating to health and safety are shared, rather than as "immoral demons of progress" at any cost. The contemporary emphasis on maintaining a positive corporate image internationally, nationally, locally, and particularly in the marketplace appears to have influenced corporate environmental policy significantly (Fischer, 1989). Clearly, some of the corporate response may be traced to morality. Further, the perception in business that profitability permits compromise and acts of reconciliation with environmental interest groups and the general public also is an important factor. This brings the question whether corporate environmental action is sacrificed in times of economic recession. Prior to the present recession, corporate executives in fact competed to demonstrate the extensiveness of their commitment to environmental concerns in some segments of industry.

It should be pointed out, however, that in the resource extraction industries, there often is far less opportunity for a meeting of preferences with interest groups in a manner that both sides perceive as ethical or equitable. The issues of property rights, acceptable levels of use or reconstitution, and definitions of what constitutes "sustainable" development, are inevitably influenced by value considerations not being amenable to compromise (Cairns, 1981; Ferguson and Ferguson, 1983; Postel and Heise, 1988; Forest Resources Commission, 1989, 1990).

The factors highlighted above appear to have influenced corporations in the development of environmental policy and planning. No claim is offered that this list is all inclusive. However, it would seem to be a first step in attempting to define a large part of the motivation for the development of corporate environmental policy over the past decade. This framework or model for understanding corporate environmental policy may be applied to evaluate the environmental performance of business in achieving publicly desired outcomes.

Corporate responsibility toward the environment is one of the most important issues in contemporary public policy. Some corporations have recognized that responsible policy towards the environment avoids legal liability and resultant costs for environmental mitigation measures. Corporations with responsible environmental policy may also achieve other benefits including reduced long-term costs for complying with government regulation and interest group pressure, and improved public image. The most prominent incentive to adopt a sound environmental policy approach for business, however, would seem to be the opportunity to convert an environmentally responsible image into increased product or service demand and greater market share and profitability.

On the larger issue of regulation and ethical behavior, the framework presented in this study suggests that ethics do play a role in causing corporations to develop environmental plans and programs. It would appear, based on the analysis presented above and evidence presented subsequently in this book, that ethical standards of behavior are reinforced by the other factors or causal variables identified in this chapter. It may be speculated that ethical standards are reinforced by corporate concerns for cost savings in management of energy and waste, by consumer demand for environmentally safe and responsible products, by interest groups that have pressured governments and corporations through the news media, and in direct lobbying to increase the allocation of resources to environmental protection and mitigation, by government environmental regulation, and by court judgments and rulings in support of the intent of regulation. Economic factors and government controls have worked to support ethical corporate behavior toward the environment. However, it is unlikely that ethical standards alone would have achieved the results produced by the combination of factors identified in this study.

One additional conclusion that may be drawn is that ethics and economics, contrary to the perceptions of many environmentalists, may work in opposite directions with regard to stimulating environmental protection. Just the opposite may be the case. The concepts and analytical techniques of economics and finance are increasingly applied to better understand the dynamics of markets so as to assist the progress of government and corporate environmentalism. Economics as a discipline may have gained a bad reputation because economists have served environmental exploiters effectively. However, the tools of the trade obviously may be applied to justify ethical environmental behavior as well. The analysis in this paper suggests that to more fully understand corporate environmentalism and the role of government in influencing corporate action, at minimum the following factors must be assessed.

- The environmental challenge to corporations.
  - The evolution of environmental thinking in society and in corporations.
  - Definitions of corporate social responsibility and responsiveness.
  - Evolving corporate environmental policy.
  - Development of corporate strategy on environmental issues.

- Corporate responses to the environmental challenge— Analysis, planning, policy.

- Analytical tools for corporate environmental policy assessment
  - economics of externalities.
  - benefit-cost analysis.
  - environmental impact and risk assessment.
  - political feasibility assessment.

- effects of environmental responsiveness on profitability (short- and long-term perspectives).
- environmental auditing and evaluation.

- Policy response options.
  - integration of environmental responsibility into corporate leadership.
  - environmental oversight: planning and forecasting, control, evaluation.
  - assessment of responsiveness impact on the organization and policy.
  - stockholder management and communications.
  - external relations management: legal and ethical issues, public opinion, community relations.
  - changing internal functions: new environmental staff responsibilities, impacts on product design and development, marketing, and sales.
  - refinement of legal approaches to environmental problems.
  - alternative environmental dispute resolution methods.
  - obtaining public and consumer support for responsible.
  - corporate environmental policies and practices.
  - Resolving employee environmentally-related problems.

- Environmental evaluation and auditing for corporations
  - Purpose of the evaluation
  - Performance of environmental evaluations and audits
  - Results of evaluations and audits and their utility

- Government environmental regulation and policy
  - Assessment of the basis for existing regulatory policy and practices
  - Direction of relevant new and proposed environmental regulation
  - Government regulatory agency enforcement policy and practices
  - Government enforcement approaches and an agenda for sponsorship of new research on environmental hazards and risks

- Corporate environmental policy and government regulatory evolution for the future

- Trends in corporate environmentalism
- Emergence of environmental marketing
- Environmentalism becomes more profitable
- Worldwide communication on corporate environmental policy
- Approaches to corporate environmental leadership
- Approaches evolving in environmental regulation.

While this book does not address all these issues, it attempts to provide a beginning point to stimulate further research.

In this regard it intends to point out that much remains to be done to stimulate improved corporate environmental policy and practices and more effective government regulation. Despite some assertions to the contrary, as a world culture and society we seem to be only at the beginning of the age of environmentalism in terms of insuring that environmental values are integrated as a significant motivating element within the international economy. This is despite the fact that the environmental "movement" in the western industrialized nations of the world is approximately 25 years old. Change in approach to environmental responsibility requires the interaction of economic, social, and cultural factors and probably cannot be implemented throughout the world by the direct action of government as much as it can be "orchestrated" by a number of parties, for example, committed individuals, biologists, engineers, anthropologists, sociologists, economists, philanthropic organizations, public interest groups, the news media, elected and appointed government officials and regulators, and public and private sector corporate decision makers. Such orchestration toward a common purpose—saving the earth and its inhabitants from destruction of the environment—will be needed in the twenty-first century to reverse the alarming trend of environmental degradation that has accompanied industrial and post-industrial development in the nineteenth and twentieth centuries. Standards of socially and scientifically acceptable behavior toward the environment appear to be a lantern that guides attempts to create a better future for the earth and its inhabitants. Chapters two, three, and four provide guidance for the development of responsible corporate environmental policy, planning, and program evaluation.

# Chapter II

# *Corporate Environmental Policy Planning and Development*

## INTRODUCTION:
## SIX STEPS TO ENVIRONMENTAL EXCELLENCE

Corporations throughout North America are developing comprehensive corporate environmental programs to address corporate environmental problems and opportunities. This movement stems from the growing recognition of the importance of environmental problems to corporate environmental officials, regulators, consumers, and investors.

Although there is considerable variation in evolving corporate programs, most tend to focus on three unifying goals:

1. To portray corporate concern and commitment about environmental issues to the public;
2. to develop a systematic program to define problems (and opportunities) and to develop policies and programs to achieve specified goals; and
3. to indicate good faith implementation.

In essence, a program must commit a company to the concepts of sustainable development; it must indicate current company status related to environmental issues (*an environmental audit*); it must indicate where the company wants to/has to go in its programs (*a corporate policy statement*); and finally, must develop a program to achieve its goals (*an action program*) (Carson and Moulder, 1991). Most environmental programs consist of the six major sequential steps summarized in Table II.1.

*Table II.1.*   Six Steps to Corporate Environmental Excellence

1. Develop program organization, staffing, and resources
2. Develop an environmental policy with full participation of corporate management
3. Accomplish an environmental audit
4. Develop an implementation program including strong technical, legal, and educational programs
5. Monitor, evaluate, and adjust the program
6. Monitor trends and support similar interests

*Source:*   Modified from Elkington and Burke (1989).

The key to development of an excellent environmental program is the issue of gathering accurate and complete internal and external information. Information is needed on pollutants; toxic and solid wastes; resources; control technologies and costs; company operations and liabilities; market trends (e.g., see *The Green Consumer*, Makower et al., 1991), and the actions of regulators and competitors.

This chapter focuses on corporate environmental policy which can vary in scope and length from a simple one-paragraph "stewardship" statement to detailed comprehensive statements of corporate beliefs, aspirations, and intentions (e.g., Alcan Aluminum's policy that covers everything from environmental assessments of investments and acquisitions to solid waste management policies).

Corporate policies can be very proactive (to prevent future problems and captive markets) or reactive (to reduce corporate liabilities and improve image). For example, corporations with significant environmental liabilities may produce a fairly reactive policy statement, choose a compliance audit and concentrate management effort on risks, liabilities, and image. Conversely, a firm seeking new markets, efficiencies, or opportunities may have a very proactive policy statement, do a comprehensive audit of operations and products, and focus management activities on cost savings and new products.

The corporate policy should be carefully developed with participation and information flow to and from all affected parties within the corporation (*Business International*, 1990). The policy must be developed with the full knowledge and participation of corporate management (the greater the involvement of the CEO and/or board the better) to provide the mandate, resources, and authority to implement the program. In summary, because the corporate policy establishes the foundation for the audit (who?, what?, and when?) and ultimately the development and implementation of the corporate action program, it is very important for top management to be involved and committed.

## THE VALDEZ PRINCIPLES

In the spring of 1989, following the Exxon Valdez oil spill in the Gulf of Alaska, a group of consumers, investors, and environmentalists formed The Coalition for Environmentally Responsible Economics (CERES) to promote a set of 10 corporate environmental management guidelines called the "Valdez Principles" (see Figure II.1).

CERES (the name of the Roman goddess of Mother Earth) is a project of the Social Investment Forum, an association of over 350 socially conscious investors controlling over $15 billion in investments. CERES called on companies to adapt the principles as corporate policy, suggesting a more favorable investment market to endorsing companies from socially responsible investors (Environmental Law Institute, March/April 1990).

The Valdez Principles cover a wide range of environmental management issues including pollution control, damage compensation, efficient use of energy and material resources, and full disclosure. The principles were introduced all over North America in stockholder meetings with 13 companies endorsing the principles so far (McCloskey, 1991; The *Washington Post*, 1991).

Although there has not been a rush of corporations embracing the Valdez Principles (attributable by many to the full disclosure requirement), the CERES effort fostered numerous related efforts worth noting. For example, the Interfaith Center on Corporate Responsibility (ICCR) filed 57 shareholder resolutions in 1990 urging companies to adopt the Valdez Principles. Similar resolutions in 1990-1991 drew record high votes at annual meetings and resulted in a number of negotiated settlements (McCloskey, 1991). In addition, in 1992, each of the Fortune 500 companies was asked to fill out a 37-page questionnaire on their corporate environmental policies and problems (The *Washington Post*, 1991).

By adopting these principles, we publicly affirm our belief that corporations and their shareholders have a direct responsibility for the environment. We believe that corporations must conduct their business as responsible stewards of the environment and seek profits only in a manner that leaves the Earth healthy and safe. We believe that corporations must not compromise the ability of future generations to sustain their needs. We recognize this to be a long-term commitment to update our practices continually in light of advances in technology and new understandings in health and environmental science. We intend to make consistent, measurable progress in implementing these principles and to apply them wherever we operate throughout the world.

**1.  Protection of the Biosphere**

We will minimize and strive to eliminate the release of any pollutant that may cause environmental damage to the air, water, or earth or its inhabitants. We will safeguard habitats in rivers, lakes, wetlands, coastal zones and oceans and will minimize contributing to the greenhouse effect, depletion of the ozone layer, acid rain, or smog.

**2.  Sustainable Use of Natural Resources**

We will make sustainable use of renewable natural resources, such as water, soils and forests. We will conserve non-renewable natural resources through efficient use and careful planning. We will protect wildlife habitats, open spaces and wilderness, while preserving biodiversity.

**3.  Reduction and Disposal of Waste**

We will minimize the creation of waste, especially hazardous waste, and wherever possible recycle materials. We will dispose of all wastes through safe and responsible methods.

**4.  Wise Use of Energy**

We will make every effort to use environmentally safe and sustainable energy sources to meet our needs. We will invest in improved energy efficiency and conservation in our operations. We will maximize the energy efficiency of products we produce and sell.

**5.  Risk Reduction**

We will minimize the environmental, health and safety risks to our employees and the communities in which we operate by employing safe technologies and operating procedures and by being constantly prepared for emergencies.

**6.  Marketing of Safe Products and Services**

We will sell products or services that minimize adverse environmental impacts and that are safe as consumers com-

monly use them. We will inform consumers of the environmental impacts of our products or services.

**7.  Damage Compensation**

We will take responsibility for any harm we cause to the environment by making every effort to fully restore the environment and to compensate those persons who are adversely affected.

**8.  Disclosure**

We will disclose to our employees and to the public incidents relating to our operations that cause environmental harm or pose health or safety hazards. We will disclose potential environmental, health or safety hazards posed by our operations, and we will not take any action against employees who report any condition that creates a danger to the environment or poses health and safety hazards.

**9.  Environmental Directors and Managers**

At least one member of the Board of Directors will be a person qualified to represent environmental interests. We will commit management resources to implement these Principles, including the funding of an office of Vice-President for Environmental Affairs or an equivalent executive position, reporting directly to the CEO, to monitor and report upon our implementation efforts.

**10.  Assessment and Annual Audit**

We will conduct and make public an annual self-evaluation of our progress in implementing these Principles and in complying with all applicable laws and regulations throughout our worldwide operations. We will work toward the timely creation of independent environmental audit procedures which we will complete annually and make available to the public.

*Source:*  (CERES, 1989)

*Figure II.1*   The Valdez Principles

# ALTERNATIVE APPROACHES TO POLICY DEVELOPMENT

This section discusses a comprehensive theoretical approach (environmental systems) and summarizes the actual practice (in two surveys) of corporate environmental policymaking. The theory section presents a set of integrated and interrelated goals, objectives and policies developed through an environmental systems perspective on corporate policy. This theoretical model is presented to provide a comprehensive and coordinated picture of a corporate policy. It represents the perspective of the physical systems that most environmental problems and opportunities involve, and is more commensurate with the ways scientists and engineers (who are usually involved in problem solving and program development) think about the natural environment. Finally, it should be noted that this is a theoretical model and that individual corporations can build their own policies using this theoretical structure—tailored to their individual needs and opportunities.

Theory:    The Environmental Systems Approach

In scientific terms, a "system" can be defined as a group of interacting components, with a defined boundary, working toward a common goal. Under this definition, a system can be one amoeba, company, community, nation, or world. Systems scientists tell us that all systems are structured and function through the interaction of mass, energy, and information. For example, a living organism comprises a multitude of organic and inorganic molecules organized in discrete cells. Its energy is obtained from the capture of solar energy and the manufacture of organic molecules whose bond energy can be used to do the work of each cell. The "information" of the organism (how to produce food, obtain energy, reproduce, etc.) is obtained both from "nature" in the form of the nucleic acids (DNA and RNA), and from "nurture" by learned behavior from perceptions and experience.

Similar relationships of mass, energy, and information can be found in all living, physical, and social systems (see outline in Attachment 5). The manner in which mass, energy, and information is handled by a system can have a profound impact on the structure and function and, therefore, the growth, perpetuation and death of that system. Although the permutations of the interactions of mass, energy, and information are almost limitless, these interactions are governed by what are called "universal natural laws." Knowledge of these laws is essential for the comprehension of the causes and consequences of environmental problems, and their management. The basic assumption is that the more a socioeconomic system is integrated with natural laws, the more stable and compatible that system will be with its surrounding as it exploits its environment for its basic needs.

The interactions of mass, energy, and information on all systems are governed by three physical laws: the *Law of Conservation of Mass* and the *First and Second Law(s) of Thermodynamics.* Scientists and engineers are taught *from day one* that these laws govern all physical interactions of the universe—with only one exception under very special conditions—Einstein's Theory of Relativity (see Miller, 1988, for further discussion).

The *Law of Conservation of Mass* simply states that mass can be neither created nor destroyed. That is, materials are never really "produced" or "consumed." They change in form from raw materials to products to wastes and residuals without a change in quantity. Thus, over time, in any stable system, the amount of matter moving into the system (e.g., resource inputs) must equal the amount of matter stored plus the amount moving out (in the form of products, pollutants and solid and toxic wastes). With knowledge of this law, engineers frequently track the movement of physical resources through productions processes looking for contaminants, leaks, inefficiencies of conversion (excess wastes), and product and waste safety issues.

Energy relationships are governed by the *First* and *Second Law(s) of Thermodynamics.* The *First Law,* "the law of conservation of energy," states that energy can neither be created or destroyed. In industrial processes, energy changes in its form (mechanical, electrical, heat) and place, but the amount of energy remains the same. Using the law of conservation of energy, engineers and ecologists track energy movement and conversions through production processes. For example, efficient energy conversions from one form to another and energy use in production processes are less expensive, polluting, and often less dangerous.

The *Second Law of Thermodynamics* or "entropy law" governs the change of form or "quality" of energy. The second law states that in any closed system the amount of energy in forms available to do useful work diminishes over time. This loss of available energy represents a diminished capacity to maintain "order" through time. Thus, in any closed system, over time, disorder (or entropy) increases.

In summary, this law tells us that to sustain or enlarge any system (e.g., a production system) requires the "expenditure" of energy. Expenditure is defined as the conversion of a "useful" form of energy (e.g., oil) to a less useful form (e.g., heat) as production work is accomplished.

In scientific terms, the entropy law is used to explain inflation, diminishing returns on investment, and the frequent shortages resulting from high levels of production and consumption of nonrenewable resources. The expenditure of increasing amounts of available energy is required to sustain production, manage shortages, or find alternatives. Similarly, as production processes get very large and complex, useful energy must be spent to protect public health, safety, and welfare from the detrimental effects of pollution, ecological disruption, or social problems that begin exceeding the ability of the environment to tolerate or assimilate.

Thus, the resource and residuals control problems addressed by corporate planners can be attributed to entropy changes, which inevitably result from the growth and development of production activities.

In summary, the challenge of the next decades involves the recognition of entropy and its origins and its management with policies of frugality, efficiency and safety (Baldwin, 1985). This law, for example, is the origin of waste management policy priorities of "reduce, reuse, recycle, and disposal."

Enough theory—Table II.2 presents a summary of a comprehensive corporate environmental policy organized into subcategories of mass, energy, and information. The table provides representative program goals and objectives and presents a comprehensive list of potential corporate actions and issues. It must be noted that this list is not all inclusive, and certain issues and actions in a natural continuum have been arbitrarily assigned to one of the categories. The categories can be flexible for policy design. In summary, this organizational system of mass (resources and residuals), energy (efficiency), and information systems is more in line with the structure and functions physical systems of the natural environment and will be more compatible with the "systems thinking" of environmental scientists and engineers.

*Table II.2.* Environmental Science-based Corporate Environmental Policy

---

I.   **GOAL**: Increase Long-Term Corporate Economic Viability by Improving Health, Safety, and Environmental Programs

II.  **OBJECTIVES**:
- Increase production efficiency—reduce costs.
- Reduce environmental impacts—decrease energy and material wastes
- Reduce insurance and legal costs and liabilities
- Improve health and safety programs
- Decrease pollution and toxic wastes
- Increase self-sufficiency
- Education—management, investors, employees, consumers, and the general public
- Improve the efficiency of corporate environmental management

III. **POLICY OUTLINE**: Health, Safety, and Environmental Policy Based on the Interactions of Mass, Energy, and Information

— Mass
- Reducing the number of material inputs into production
- Reduce and reuse of toxic inputs
- Effective and efficient waste collection, storage, and disposal
- Product and packaging modification for safety, efficiency of resource inputs (e.g., increasing volume and concentration per product unit, recyclability (materials and mixtures), and biodegradability
- Increased use of recycled materials
- Promote public and private recycling programs
- Define and market a line of "green" products

— Energy
- Energy-efficient processes and product designs
- Facility self-reliance
- Energy end-use matching—appropriate forms

— Information
- Assignment of administrative responsibility
- Policy analysis and development
- Environmental auditing and monitoring
- Risk assessment and management
- Regulatory compliance and enforcement
- Altenative dispute resolution
- Cost(s) internalization—accounting
- Research and development
- Emergency response

- Education—management, investors, employees, consumers, and the public
- Facility siting and design
- Employee health and safety programs
- Substance abuse — tobacco, alcohol, and drugs
- Health — exercise/wellness programs
- Safety training and information
- Health insurance
- Transportation
- Consumer programs—information and service
- Annual reporting

## Practice:   Surveys of Corporate Environmental Policies

The purpose of this section is to provide corporate environmental managers with descriptive materials on real (not theoretical) existing corporate policies. This section will overview the findings of two surveys taken in 1990 of the environmental goals, policies, and implementation strategies of major corporations and will summarize the state of practice in several of corporate endeavor.

The first survey, published in January of 1990, was conducted by the Environmental Policy Center in Washington, DC, for the Business Roundtable and is entitled "Issues Addressed by Existing Corporate Policies in Health Safety and the Environment."

The Environmental Policy Center reviewed policy statements from 27 Business Roundtable companies. The survey found 21 major issues common to the corporate policy statements that were grouped in four major themes (Table II.3). (summarized by Snyder, 1991) presents the themes and common policies. The survey concludes with company-specific policies for each of the 21 issues. This information could be quite useful to managers currently involved in writing environmental policy statements.

The purpose of the second survey profiled, entitled "Corporate Environmental Policies Report" by the Environmental Law Institute (October 3, 1990), is to provide environmental managers with descriptive materials on the general goals, program objectives, and implementing mechanisms of the environmental policies of 71 companies from 15 business or industry sectors.

The report also briefly addresses the role of trade associations in developing an environmental policy and gives examples of corporate and trade association policies in appendices.

*Table II.3.* Themes and Issues Common to 27 Corporate Environmental Policies

I. **Make a fundamental commitment to sound environmental, health, and safety practices**
1. Health, safety, and the environment are priorities in evaluating and planning product, process, service, and other business decisions.
2. Protect environmental quality and human welfare in our communities. Implement environmentally sound policies designed to prevent, mitigate, and, where appropriate, remediate impacts on the health, safety, and envirobment of the community.
3. Provide and maintain a safe and healthy work environment for employees.
4. Counsel customers on potential health and environmental hazards and work with them to address questions and concerns.
5. Communicate and instill an organizational commitment to health, safety, and environmental protection throughout the company, Ensure that all levels of the organization should understand their responsibility for implementing environmental and safety practices.

II. **Contribute commitment and experience to broader-based efforts**
6. Be proactive in promoting sound environmental principles and practices throughout industry, including by sharing expereince and expertise with others.
7. Establish and nurture open communications with the community and employees. Be responsibe to community concerns about business decisions, such as land development; manufacturing operations; and the storage, release, or disposal of hazardous materials.
8. Foster a cosntructive working environment with other interested parties, such as environmental organizations, international business, and environmental groups, as well as with governments.
9. Actively participate in the development of sound environmental, health, and safety laws, regulations and policies, working with government and other interested parties.
10. Recognize the international dimensions of environmental concerns and support efforts to develop international cooperation solutions.
11. Apply sound health, safety, and environmental management practices in facilities, operations and dealings worldwide to the extent practicable given the laws, culture, and other particular characteristics of the host country.

III. **Commit to understanding and addressing concerns underlying environmental, health, and safety laws and regulations**
12. Put in place policies, programs, and procedures, as well as the letter, or laws and regulations. This includes establishing goals and targets against which progress can be measured.
13. Conduct periodic health, safety, and environmental reviews to evaluate environmental and safety performance, measuring progress against goals and targets. Take steps to correct any deficiencies and identify areas for improvement.

14. Make sure that employees are informed of envronemtnal requirements and trained as needed to implement safety measures.

IV. **Expand efforts to improve protectiona nd conservation beyond what is required**

15. Develop and implement environmentally safe practices whenever possible even in the absence of governmental standards or other regulations.
16. Minimize the generation of discharges to the environment, including but not limited to hazardous and nonhazardous waste.
17. Develop sound waste management practices.
18. Commit to recycling to preserve natural resouces and reduce disposal burden.
19. Commit to the wise use of energy by improving energy efficiency.
20. Recognize and encourage the contribution every employee can make toward improved safety and environmental performance.
21. Endorse and support research aimed at improving knowledge on and capability to eliminate and mitigate risks such as research on health, safety and environmental effects on process safety, pollution control technologies, and safet alternatives. The report also briefly addresses the role of trade associations in developing an environmental policy and gives examples of corporate and trade associations policies and appendices.

*Source:* The Environmental Policy Center (1990).

Table II.4 summarizes the goals, objectives, and implementing mechanisms identified by the Environmental Law Institute Report.

Attachments 1-4 to this paper present the policy statements for the American Petroleum Institute, the Chemical Manufacturers' Association, the First Interstate Bank and the National Association of Manufacturers. One of the best utility environmental policy statements in North America comes from Alberta's TransAlta Utilities Corporation. Table II.5 summarizes the TransAlta statement (Carson and Moulder, 1991).

## Case Studies

The number and nature of corporate environmental Policies preclude an in-depth presentation of case studies of corporate environmental policies. The two major survey reports cited in the previous section provide several excellent examples of corporate and manufacturing association policy statements. One excellent recent publication (March 1991) was produced by Industry, Science and Technology Canada entitled "Competitiveness in the '90s

*Table II.4.*    Goals, Objectives, and Implementing Mechanisms of the Environmental Law Institute Report

I.    **General Goals:** A broad standard that a company expects its environmental performance to meet or exceed. Some company policies include only goals, while others include more specific objectives, and a few—implementing mechanisms.

1.    Compliance with the Law—one of the most common objectives—includes legal categories (e.g., pollution, health) and coverage of subsidiaries and foreign operations.

2.    Environmental Protection—most common standard found; often serves as the cornerstone of a company's environmental policy.

●    Risk Management—minimizing or eliminating the risk of harm to the environment or human health from pollution was one of the most common variations on the theme of environmental protection.

●    Environmental Stewardship—another variation on the environmental protection theme that includes protection of the environment, particularly the companies' natural resources, in a morally, ethically, or socially responsible manner for present and future generations.

3.    Leadership—the concept of social or industry leadership implies exemplary or innovative behavior and is thus distinct from the concept of environmental stewardship.

4.    Public Responsiveness—this standard involves a company recognizing and satisfying public or customer concerns about its environmental performance.

II.    Program Objectives: A specific environmental objective that a company believes is fundamental to achieving its broad environmental goals.

**General Program Objectives**

1.    Source Reduction—reduction and/or elimination of the generation, discharge, and/or use of a potential pollutant or waste.

2.    Proper Treatment, Storage, Transportation, and Disposal—implicitly acknowledges that in some industries it is impossible to eliminate or recycle pollution or waste generated or used by the industry, but provides for a commitment by the company to take proper steps to protect the public and/or the environment from the harmful or negative effects that could occur in the treatment, storage, transportation, or disposal of such pollution or waste.

3.    Conservation of Natural Resources—many variations: utilizing natural resources efficiently, using natural resources in a sustainable manner, using renewable resources, and carefully managing resources.

4.    Product Stewardship—involves the incorporation of environmental, and commonly health and safety, consideration in the planning, design production and distribution of a product.

**Specialized Program Objectives**—focus on a specific environment or company program.

1. Ground water protection
2. Surface water protection
3. Air emmissions reduction
4. Biological diversity
5. Energy efficiency
6. Preferential or integrated waste/pollution management systems.

III. **Implementing Mechanisms:** The practices and procedures a company uses to achieve its program objectives or general goals. These may be published in employer manuals, in separate implementation program documents, or as part of the corporate policy.

**Common Implementing Mechanisms**—Found in many corporate policies.

1. Development of Internal Standards—the thrust of these principles is a commitment to develop internal company standards for protection of the environment on aspects where no laws or regulations exist or where existing laws or regulations do not go far enough. They may also come into play when a company is operating in a country that does not have adequate environmental protection laws.

2. Assignment of Responsibility—falls into two categories: those that assign general responsibility to all employees and those that assign specific responsibilities to different levels of management and/or employees.

3. Recycling—commonly address internal recycling programs of waste materials; industries that are involved in the production of potentially recyclable products or products with potentially recyclable packaging tend to have principles that support efforts to encourage public recycling through the use and production of recyclable products and packaging, coding of recyclable products and packaging, and participation in public recycling efforts, research, and education.

4. Assessment of Environmental Impact—Falls into two categories: those that require consideration of environmental factors in the planning and development of a company's products, processes and/ or facilities and those that require consideration of environmental factors in connection with the acquisition, leasing sale and/or divesture of company property.

5. Communication and Training—addressed to employees and/or members of the public and generally seek to protect those persons from environmental safety and or health hazards associated with a company's products or operations by the provision of information or training.

6. Remediation—a commitment by a company to take responsibility for and correct environmental, health, or safety problems resulting from its past or future actions.

7. Communication and Cooperation to Develop Environmental Standards and Solutions—address outreach efforts by a company to the community, the government, trade associations, and/or public

*(continued)*

*Table II.4.* Continued

---

interest groups to develop public policies, programs, and laws protective of the environment.

8. Environmental Compliance Programs—a commitment by a company to conduct some type of review and/or self-monitoring program that will assure compliance of a company's operations with the company's environmental policy or applicable laws or regulations; one of the most popular programs specifically referenced for assuring environmental compliance is the environmental audit.

9. Research and Development—a commitment to conduct or support internal or external research and development programs for environmentally protective products or technology.

10. Commitment of Resources—a general commitment to provide the resources necessary to implement a company's environmental policy.

11. Changing or Eliminating Products or Processes—a commitment to discontinue any or certain hazardous or harmful processes or products.

12. Contractor Compliance—a commitment to monitor performance of independent contractors working for the company for compliance with a company's environmental policy or applicable laws and regulations, and to select for use by the company only those contractors whose performance meets such standards.

**Specialized Implementing Mechanisms**—Found in a specific industry or small number of companies.

1. Specific product or process changes
2. High-level corporate involvement with policy violations
3. Encouraging and rewarding positive employee performance
4. Disciplining employee violations
5. Goal setting
6. Prompt response to environmental problems
7. Secondary uses of property
8. Environmentally beneficial technology and product applications
9. Prioritizing of environmental issues
10. Supporting public transportation
11. Supporting environmental organizations
12. Specific research and development projects
13. Defining criteria for "unacceptable risks"
14. Defining criteria for "environmentally friendly" product packaging
15. Supporting community recycling programs
16. Employing best control methods
17. Annual environmental performance report

---

Environmental Performance," which profiles the environmental policies, programs, and lessons learned from 11 companies in British Columbia.

*Table II.5.*   The TransAlta Utilities Corporation Environmental Policy Statement

---

TransAlta is committed to the protection of the environment and to sustainable development. Environmental stewardship is a vital element in our business. We strive to empower all our employees to take initiative to protect and enhance the environment, based on shared values and the need to satisfy the environmental concerns and expectations of customers, investors, and the public. Our commitments are to:

---

- Report complete and accurate information on the environmental impact of our business, meet or surpass all environmental standards, and continuously improve our environmental performance.
- Advocate socially responsible environmental standards and the recognition of the economic value of environmental resources.
- Implement conservation and efficiency initiatives for all resources and pursue alternative energy opportunities, both within our own operations and in partnership with others.
- Seek out research operations and develop alliances that will improve our environmental performance and make a positive contribution to solving environmental challenges.
- Consult and work cooperatively with those who may be affected by our business and respond to their environmental concerns.
- Recognize and respect the relationship between environment and health in all phases of our business, and use the best knowledge available to protect the health of employees and the public.
- Encourage the development of educational programs and resources, to provide balanced public information and to foster environmentally sensitive attitudes, knowledge, and skills.
- Identify and develop business ventures where value can be added to environmental solutions while providing investment opportunities for the corporation and its shareholders.

---

*Source:*   Crason and Moulder (1991).

# CONCLUSION

In summary, a corporate environmental policy can range from a simple goal statement to a complex set of goals, objectives, and implementing mechanisms. It is very important to the corporate environment program to carefully develop these policies early in the program evolution to help access program resource needs, establish lines of authority and communications, legitimize the management plan and to establish the foundation for audits, plan development, and implementation.

As indicated in this chapter, very useful and informative resources are available to the corporate manager for policy development. In addition, many business organizations are engaged in on-going information gathering or major studies of environmental policy development. Most notable is the United States Corporate Conservation Council (a group of senior corporate executives working with representatives of the World Wildlife Fund) and Canada's Business Council on National Issues (BCNI) that has asked its Environmental Task Force to prepare a report to profile companies on the leading edge of the corporate environmental movement (Carson and Moulder, 1991).

Attachments to follow

*Attachment 1*

# American Petroleum Institute
# Environmental Principles

*The members of the American Petroleum Institute are dedicated to continuous efforts to improve the compatibility of our operations with the environment while economically developing energy resources and supplying high-quality products and services to consumers. The members recognize the importance of efficiently meeting society's needs and our responsibility to work with the public, the government, and others to develop and to use natural resources in an environmentally sound manner while protecting the health and safety of our employees and the public. To meet these responsibilities, API members pledge to manage our businesses according to these principles:*

**PRINCIPLES**

- To recognize and to respond to community concerns about our raw materials, products and operations.

- To operate our plants and facilities, and to handle our raw materials and products in a manner that protects the environment, and the safety and health of our employees and the public.

- To make safety, health and environmental considerations a priority in our planning, and our development of new products and processes.

- To advise promptly appropriate officials, employees, customers and the public of information on significant industry-related safety, health and environmental hazards, and to recommend protective measures.

- To counsel customers, transporters and others in the safe use, transportation and disposal of our raw materials, products and waste materials.

- To economically develop and produce natural resources and to conserve those resources by using energy efficiently.

- To extend knowledge by conducting or supporting research on the safety, health and environmental effects of our raw materials, products, processes and waste materials.

- To commit to reduce overall emissions and waste generation.

- To work with others to resolve problems created by handling and disposal of hazardous substances from our operations.

- To participate with government and others in creating responsible laws, regulations and standards to safeguard the community, workplace and environment.

- To promote these principles and practices by sharing experiences and offering assistance to others who produce, handle, use, transport or dispose of similar raw materials, petroleum products and wastes.

*Attachment 1.* Continued

American
Petroleum
Institute

# American Petroleum Institute
# Our Mission, Values, Objectives

| MISSION | *The American Petroleum Institute (API) is the U.S. petroleum industry's primary trade association. API provides public policy development and advocacy, research and technical services to enhance the ability of the petroleum industry to meet its mission which includes:* |
|---|---|

- meeting the nation's energy needs, developing energy sources, and supplying high-quality products and services;

- enhancing the environmental, health, and safety performance of the petroleum industry; and

- conducting research to advance petroleum technology and develop industry equipment and performance standards.

*In performing our mission, API advocates government decision-making that encourages efficient and economic oil and natural gas development, refining, transportation, and use; API promotes an improved public understanding of the industry's value to society; and API serves as a forum for the exchange of views on issues affecting the petroleum industry.*

**VALUES**

*We hold these core values:*

- *Performance.* Our effectiveness depends upon the performance of the men and women who make up API. They are the key to our success.

- *Excellence.* We are committed to excellence in serving the petroleum industry. We will do everything possible to meet or, wherever possible, exceed the industry's needs.

- *Highest Standards.* We will adhere to the highest ethical and professional standards. We must do so in order to achieve the public credibility that is key to our success.

**OBJECTIVES**

*We are committed to achieving these objectives:*

- *Continuously improve the quality and the value of the services we provide.* We are committed to being an industry asset widely respected for providing services that meet high standards of excellence. We will anticipate and respond quickly to the changing needs of both our members and our staff.

- *Strive for excellence and efficiency in our operations.* We will maintain the respect of our members through employee initiative, improved productivity, and cost-effectiveness.

- *Foster team spirit among employees.* We will provide a work environment built on open communication, teamwork, trust, and personal development and recognition.

*Attachment 2*

Guiding Principles for

# RESPONSIBLE CARE

## A Public Commitment

As a member of the Chemical Manufacturers Association, this company is committed to support a continuing effort to improve the industry's responsible management of chemicals. We pledge to manage our business according to these principles:

■ To recognize and respond to community concerns about chemicals and our operations.

■ To develop and produce chemicals that can be manufactured, transported, used and disposed of safely.

■ To make health, safety and environmental considerations a priority in our planning for all existing and new products and processes.

■ To report promptly to officials, employees, customers and the public, information on chemical-related health or environmental hazards and to recommend protective measures.

■ To counsel customers on the safe use, transportation and disposal of chemical products.

■ To operate our plants and facilities in a manner that protects the environment and the health and safety of our employees and the public.

■ To extend knowledge by conducting or supporting research on the health, safety and environmental effects of our products, processes and waste materials.

■ To work with others to resolve problems created by past handling and disposal of hazardous substances.

■ To participate with government and others in creating responsible laws, regulations and standards to safeguard the community, workplace and environment.

■ To promote the principles and practices of Responsible Care by sharing experiences and offering assistance to others who produce, handle, use, transport or dispose of chemicals.

*Attachment 3*

# THE FIRST INTERSTATE POLICY ON THE ENVIRONMENT

First Interstate Bank believes that our society's best interests depend upon sound economic growth which is vitally linked to a healthy natural environment. The bank is therefore dedicated, in its business policies and practices, to demonstrating its commitment to environmental protection by balancing the needs of the present with those of the future.

The bank's policy is to:

- Manage all aspects of our business in ways that acknowledge environmental concerns as well as economic realities;

- Manage our internal operations in ways that will conserve our natural resources by reducing consumption and reusing and recycling materials wherever feasible;

- Establish plans and procedures aimed at integrating this policy into our daily working life—enhancing, expanding, or initiating programs as needed and periodically assessing our progress;

- Provide support through its program of charitable contributions to selected non-profit groups who are active in the areas of conservation and preservation of the environment and wildlife;

- Continue to give appropriate consideration to environmental laws and risks in assessing proposed loans and investments, and in managing our assets;

- Encourage our employees to be protective of the environment at work, at home, and in the community;

- Communicate our environmental policy and actions to our customers and investors, as well as to our employees and vendors.

*Attachment 4*

**PROPOSED NAM RECOMMENDED ENVIRONMENTAL GUIDELINE**

The National Association of Manufacturers believes that all companies should articulate and implement their commitments to health, safety and the environment. As such, NAM offers the following as suggestions for those companies that wish to develop, reaffirm or strengthen such guidelines:

GOBAL STATEMENT: Many existing policies include a global statement to express (i) a general commitment to health, safety and the environment that frames more specific commitments, and/or (ii) support for broad human welfare and environmental conservation issues which can not be addressed by direct, identifiable company commitments. This is an example of such a statement:

XYZ recognizes and believes in the importance of safeguarding natural resources and the global environmental heritage, including wildlife habitants and biological diversity. We are committed to our employees, our customer and our communities; their health, safety, and their understanding of the need for each individual's environmental stewardship. We believe that health, safety and environmental goals can and should be consistent with economic health.

Make a fundamental commitment to sound environmental, health and practices
1) Health, safety and the environment are priorities in evaluating and planning product, process, service and other business decisions.
2) Protect environmental quality and human welfare in our communities. Implement environmentally sound policies designed to prevent, mitigate and, where appropriate, remediate impacts on the health, safety and environment of the community.
3) Provide and maintain a safe and healthy work environment for employees.
4) Counsel customers on potential health and environmental hazards and work with them to address questions and concerns.
5) Communicate and instill an organizational commitment to health, safety and environmental protection throughout the company. Ensure that all levels of the organization should understand their responsibility and accountability for implementing environmental and safety practices.

Contribute commitment and experience to broader-based efforts
6) Be proactive in promoting sound environment principles and practices throughout industry, including by sharing experience and expertise with others.
7) Establish and nurture open communications with the community and employees. Be responsive to community concerns about business decisions such as land development, manufacturing operations, and the storage or disposal of hazardous materials.
8) Foster a constructive working environment with other interested parties such as environmental organizations, international business and environmental groups, as well as with governments.

*(continued)*

## *Attachment 4* Continued

9) Actively participate in the development of sound environmental, health and safety laws, regulations and policies, working with government and other interested parties.

10) Recognize the international dimensions of environmental concerns and support efforts to develop international cooperation and solutions.

11) Apply sound health, safety and environmental management practices in facilities, operations and dealings world-wide to the extent practicable given the laws, culture and other particular characteristics of the host country.

Commit to understanding and addressing concerns underlying environmental, health and safety laws and regulations

12) Put in place policies, programs and procedures as well as internal controls to ensure compliance with the spirit, as well as the letter, of laws and regulations. This includes establishing goals and targets against which progress can be measured.

13) Conduct periodic health, safety and environmental reviews to evaluate environmental and safety performance, measuring progress against goals and targets. Take steps to correct any deficiencies and identify areas for improvement.

14) Make sure that employees are informed of environmental requirements and trained as needed to implement safety measures.

Expand efforts to improve protection and conservation beyond what is required

15) Develop and implement environmentally safe practices whenever possible even int he absence of governmental standards or other regulations.

16) Minimize the generation of discharges to the environment including, but not limited to, hazardous and non-hazardous waste.

17) Develop sound waste management practices.

18) Commit to the wise use of energy by improving energy efficiency.

19) Commit to the wise use of energy by improving energy efficiency.

20) Recognize and encourage the contribution every employee can make toward improved safety and environmental performance.

21) Endorse and support research aimed at improving knowledge on and capability to eliminate and mitigate risks such as research on health, safety and environmental effects and on process safety, pollution control technologies and safer alternatives.

## Attachment 5

### CORPORATE ENVIRONMENTAL POLICY

I.  GOAL: Increase Long-term Corporate Economic Viability by Improving Health, Safety and Environmental Programs

II. OBJECTIVES:

- Increase Production Efficiency – Reduce Costs
- Reduce Environmental Impacts – Decrease Energy and Material Wastes
- Reduce Insurance and Legal Costs and Liabilities:
  - Improve Health and Safety Programs
  - Decrease Pollution and Toxic Wastes
- Increase Self-sufficiency
- Education – Management, Investors, Employees, Consumers and the General Public
- Improve the Efficiency of Corporate Environmental Management

III. POLICY OUTLINE: Health, Safety and Environmental Policy Based on the Interactions of Mass, Energy, and Information.

1. Mass
   - Reducing the number of material inputs into production
   - Reduce and reuse of toxic inputs
   - Effective and efficient waste collection, storage and disposal
   - Product and packaging modification for safety, efficiency of resource inputs (e.g., increasing volume and concentration per product unit), recyclability (materials and mixtures) and biodegradability
   - Increased use of recycled materials
   - Promote public and private recycling programs
   - Define and market a line of "green" products
2. Energy
   - Energy efficient processes and product designs
   - Facility self reliance
   - Energy end-use matching – appropriate forms
   - Waste heat utilization
3. Information
   - Assignment of administrative responsibility
   - Policy analysis and development
     - Environmental auditing and monitoring
     - Risk assessment and management
     - Regulatory compliance and enforcement
     - Alternative dispute resolution
     - Cost(s) internalization – accounting
   - Emergency response
   - Education – management, investors, employees, consumers and the public
   - Facility siting and design
   - Employee health and safety programs
     - Substance abuse – tobacco, alcohol and drugs
     - Health – exercise/wellness programs
     - Health insurance
     - Transportation
   - Consumer programs – information and service
   - Annual reporting

11) Apply sound health, safety and environmental management practices in facilities, operations and dealings world-wide to the extent practicable given the laws, culture and other particular characteristics of the host country.

**Commit to understanding and addressing concerns underlying environmental, health and safety laws and regulations**

12) Put in place policies, programs and procedures as well as internal controls to ensure compliance with the spirit, as well as the letter, of laws and regulations. This includes establishing goals and targets against which progress can be measured.

13) Conduct periodic health, safety and environmental reviews to evaluate environmental and safety performance, measuring progress against goals and targets. Take steps to correct any deficiencies and identify areas for improvement.

14) Make sure that employees are informed of environmental requirements and trained as needed to implement safety measures.

**Expand efforts to improve protection and conservation beyond what is required**

15) Develop and implement environmentally safe practices whenever possible even in the absence of governmental standards or other regulations.

16) Minimize the generation of discharges to the environment including, but not limited to, hazardous and non-hazardous waste.

17) Develop sound waste management practices.

18) Commit to recycling to preserve natural resources and reduce disposal burden.

19) Commit to the wise use of energy by improving energy efficiency.

20) Recognize and encourage the contribution every employee can make toward improved safety and environmental performance.

21) Endorse and support research aimed at improving knowledge on and capability to eliminate and mitigate risks such as research on health, safety and environmental effects and on process safety, pollution control technologies and safer alternatives.

# Chapter III

# *Evaluating Corporate Environmental Performance*

## INTRODUCTION

### Background

An environmental audit is defined as a basic management tool involving a systematic, documented, periodic, and objective evaluation of how well corporate environmental organization, management, and technological systems are performing. The basic aim of an environmental audit is to facilitate management control of environmental practices, and to assess compliance with company policies and external regulatory requirements (ICC, 1988; UNEP, 1988).

According to the United Nation's Environmental Program (UNEP, 1988, p. 2):

> In essence, environmental audits should not be undertaken simply to facilitate compliance with the law; they should be seen as a means to accomplish much more in as much as they provide an in-depth review of company processes and progress in realizing long-term strategic goals. One great advantage of regular auditing is that it provides the company with a greater overall awareness of its workers and processes, identifying compliance problems and areas of risk, pinpointing both strengths and weaknesses, and encouraging continual improvement. In that regard environmental auditing encourages the use of low-waste technologies, prudent utilization of resources and identification of potential hazards and risks.

Environmental auditing first appeared in the early 1970s, largely among companies operating in environmentally intensive sectors such as petroleum and industrial chemicals. Since that time, environmental auditing has steadily increased in popularity because of:

- *Industrial Accidents* and their political and economic sequences (e.g., Basle, Bhopol, Chernobyl, Exxon-Valdez).
- *Regulatory Controls* that continually change, become more specific and vary from country to country.
- *Public Awareness* of growing environmental problems and their ecological and human health consequences.
- *Litigation*—the increase in liability and litigation necessitate management control because of legal management responsibility.

As the environmental audit has evolved into a useful and popular management tool, experience has provided insights into successful auditing approaches. For example, in developing an audit, several issues must be addressed, including: corporate goals and philosophy; the type, tools, and reporting methods of the audit; selection of the auditors; pre-audit preparation and post-audit communications and implementation, to make an audit a success. The International Chamber of Commerce has published some useful guidelines for environmental auditing (ICC, 1988; ICC, 1989). These will be incorporated into this chapter.

The requirements for environmental audits, however, vary considerably from company to company according to the nature of the business, the regulatory climate, past and present management practices, and current corporate goals and philosophy. Therefore, this paper will also provide an overview of the breadth of options available and flexibility within the formal audit process to meet the diverse needs of individual companies.

In summary, several hundred major corporations in Canada, Europe, and the United States have established formal audit programs designed to provide senior management with assurance that operations and products are being managed and produced in accordance with established governmental standards and good industry practice (Hedstrom and Obbagy, 1988).

*Table III.1.* Benefits of an Environmental Audit

- Safeguard health and the environment
- Verify compliance with state and federal environmental laws
  - keep informed of legal changes
  - decrease liability of management
- Verify compliance with corporate policies and standards
- Indicate current or future problems and/or risks that should be addressed
- Reduce corporate exposure to litigation, accidents, and adverse publicity
- Assess corporate liabilities in takeovers, expansions, and use of subsidiaries and independent contractors
- Produce better, safer, cheaper, more competitive products
- Evaluate alternative methods of remediation and environmental impact assessment and management
- Stay informed of technical advances in pollution control
- Improve corporate environmental performance by highlighting improvements and deficiencies
- Identify cost and hazards reduction
- Increase employee/management awareness of environmental problems
- Assess and provide information for worker education programs
- Provide an environmental database for reporting, planning, plant modification, emergency responses, program evaluation and modification, and employee education
- Demonstrate corporate environmental commitment to employees, authorities, stockholders, investors, and the public

*Source:* *Business International,* (1990), Tusa (1990)

## Goals and Objectives of an Environmental Audit

The increasing popularity of the environmental audit as a tool for corporate management is reflected in the number and nature of benefits potentially realized in the number and nature of benefits potentially realized by a company auditing its business practices. In general, an environmental audit can improve profits (by cutting liabilities, increasing operation efficiencies, and identifying new market opportunities); reduce environmental impacts, risks, and liabilities; improve corporate emergency and market responsiveness; and can help to enhance corporate image. Table III.1 provides a more detailed summary of the corporate benefits of an environmental audit.

## TYPICAL ENVIRONMENTAL AUDIT PROCESS

Environmental audits have many different objectives, are conducted in a variety of settings, and by audit teams of varied background and experience. However, audits often focus on several key company operations and follow a fairly common set of processes and procedures (an "audit protocol"). This section briefly overviews a basic audit protocol and emphasizes flexibility and alternatives possible within the formal structure (UNEP, 1988).

A typical audit usually involves three interrelated (and periodically repeated) phases; a pre-audit; a site visit and analysis; and post-audit reporting and program implementation (see Figure III.1). This uniform, formal structure of the protocol is used to assure adequate, accurate coverage of products, and operations and to facilitate future replicability.

### Pre-Audit Activities

Pre-audit activities include a number of functions preparatory to the actual site visit and analysis. These include a review of all available information and applicable environmental rules and regulations, previous audit reports and information on the policies, processes, facilities, and products of the host company.

Pre-audit activities should also establish lines of responsibility and communication and to assess and organize the resources for completing the site visit and analysis and reporting and implementing findings.

Pre-audit activities often result in the development of an audit plan which defines the technical, geographic, cost, resource, and chronological scope of the audit. Three issues that are critical in carefully developing the audit plan are the corporate environmental commitment (through policy statements or program elements); determination of the needs of the company (to be addressed in a specific type of audit) and the choice of the auditing team, tools, and processes. These three issues warrant further discussion.

### Corporate Education Policy and Commitment

If auditing is new to a company (or a subsidiary), there is a great need for education of those involved in the process (the auditors and the auditees). Educational materials on the purpose of the corporate environmental program, related policies, audit procedures and alternatives, and program implementation can be

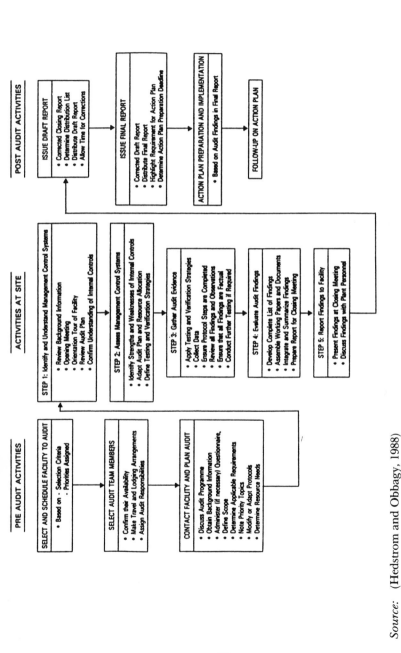

*Figure III.1.* Basic Steps of an Environmental Audit

*Source:* (Hedstrom and Obbagy, 1988)

49

very useful in program development. This information tends to alleviate fears, and foster cooperation among employees or managers—through an understanding of the motives, benefits, and procedures for program development (*Business International,* 1990).

One of the most important pre-audit activities of a company is the development and formal adoption of a corporate "environmental policy" statement, specifying corporate environmental goals and objectives. This, in turn, forms the basis for the environmental audit (who, what, and where) and ultimately the design and implementation of a management program.

Corporate policies vary widely by company history, processes, and products. In general, however, a corporate policy often addresses several critical issues (Tusa, 1990):

- Risk assessment and management;
- Environmental management program evaluation;
- Forecasting futures for opportunities and preventative measures;
- Minimize environmental damage and liabilities;
- Enhance corporate image; and
- Protect senior management.

As mentioned in the previous chapter, corporate policies can be very proactive (to prevent future problems and captive markets) or reactive (to reduce corporate liabilities and improve image).

In summary, the policy statement sets the agenda for the audit and management effort. Thus, it is very important for top management to be involved and committed in the development of a corporate environmental policy—to initiate program development.

## Types of Audits

There are many different types of audits and it is important to be clear as to what exactly the audit will cover and to what depth. This section will summarize and discuss some of the different types of audits.

The first main differential is between internal and external environmental auditing. An internal environmental audit is designed to get your own house in order with a minimum of outside interference (or objective evaluation). An external environmental audit is an independent means of evaluating performance, internal audits, and/or "fine tuning" management and operational procedures to achieve an optimum in environmental management. The major types of audits are:

*Corporate Audit.* A comprehensive corporate audit of policies, programs, facilities, processes, and products.

*Management Audit.* This is an audit of corporate environmental administration, including administrative roles and responsibilities, personnel policies, communications (open and operational), and availability of necessary financial and technical resources for effective environmental management.

*Issues Audit.* An issues audit is an analysis of a company's contribution to a specific environmental problem (e.g., solid waste, pollution, toxins, deforestation) or opportunity (e.g., site restoration or habitat enhancement). The audit usually focuses on a specific issue from the standpoint of goals/objectives, policies/guidelines, and practices and procedures.

*Emerging Issues Audit.* Monitoring and assessing new issues important to corporate environmental affairs (e.g., public opinion, green consumerism, investor behavior) and developing appropriate response alternatives.

*Operations Audit.* An assessment of the environmental effects of a particular operation (e.g., electroplating, refining, toxic chemical production) of a company.

*Technical Audit.* A technical audit is an analysis of company resources (land, labor, and capital), processes (e.g., energy consumption, site analysis, pollution control technology) and products.

*Compliance Audit.* A simple audit to assess company compliance with the minimum legal local, state, and federal standards to protect human health and the environment. This may include compliance with more stringent company standards.

*Loss Control Audit.*   A loss control audit identifies, assesses, and prioritizes all legal, financial, political, risk, health, and environmental liabilities of a company. The result is an annual updated list of priority issues for management actions.

*Site Audit.*   A site audit is an audit of a particular facility believed to be problematic.

*Associate Audit.*   An associate audit analyzes the environmental programs of a subsidiary, supplier, or subcontractor.

*Pre-acquisition Audit.*   A pre-acquisition audit is an assessment of a facility or company prior to acquisition. The audit identifies actual or potential problems, and takes these into account in final negotiations for acquisition.

*Pre-sale Audits.*   A pre-sale audit is an audit conducted by an owner of a company prior to sale to remedy environmental problems (to improve salability) and to establish a baseline against which future issues of liability can be assessed. Sources: *Business International,* 1990; Elkington, 1990; ICC, 1989; Jackson, 1990; Maxwell, 1990; Shea, 1989; Tusa, 1990; UNEP, 1990.

## Auditors, Tools, and Processes

A skilled, knowledgable, and unbiased auditing team is essential for a successful audit. The team should be familiar with the type of company being audited (or the specific facility)—its processes and products, technical and environmental controls, pertinent environmental risks and regulations, and should be relatively independent financially from the audited company (Tusa, 1990).

There are two basic approaches to team selection, internal and external, with both having relative advantages and disadvantages. An internally recruited team can be the cheapest, fastest, and most "secure." An interdisciplinary team of company legal, financial, technical, and managerial representatives can be assembled and given the task of producing an audit report. An internal team has the advantage of insiders knowledge of processes and products and can provide friendly, familiar faces to encourage company cooperation. The disadvantages of such an approach are in objectivity (and therefore accuracy) created by internal biases and fear of reprisals from company superiors or colleagues (Tusa, 1990).

An external audit, on the other hand, is more costly and time-consuming, yet often is more objective and accurate because of the previously mentioned concerns. External audits are usually contracted out, based on an "audit plan" to an experienced consulting firm. It is often advisable to have one trusted facility representative on, or working for, the auditing team to answer questions to the auditors, provide a liaison with the company and give the auditing team a familiar face to foster employee cooperation.

Once the auditing team has been selected, auditing procedures and products or "audit tools"—are developed to evaluate and report the findings of the audit. The "tools" usually consist of a notification form, an audit manual, checklists, and a specified report format and process.

The *notification form* provides company management and employees with information on the purpose and intent of the audit, its schedule, the membership of the auditing team and its authority and the nature of the information to be collected. The notification form should be sent to facilities or departments that are to be audited giving them sufficient time to gather and organize pertinent information.

The *auditing manual* is a reference guide for management and team members to assure program accuracy, consistency, and replicatability (in future years). The manual usually contains the corporate environmental policy statement, the type(s) of audit to be accomplished, a summary of the audit team and selection process, procedures for accomplishing the audit, templates for audit preparation, applicable rules and regulations, a schedule of future auditing intervals, and issue *checklists*. These checklists tend to be lists of questions or issues to be answered or addressed by each department in fulfilling audit requirements. Checklists are provided to assure the audit is comprehensive, with no important issues overlooked (Tusa, 1990).

Once the audit data has been collected, organized, and interpreted, a number of *report formats* are possible for relaying information to management. These can range from group meeting oral reports to summary checklists of issues (and corresponding actions) to full-blown annual reports—depending on the wishes of the host company (Tusa, 1990).

## The Environmental Audit

*Process.*   An environmental audit involves close examination of site activities and identifying areas for improvement of specified goals. The process usually involves: (1)   an introductory step to provide information on facilities and auditing processes, (2)   the collection of information, (3)   the evaluation of that information (against specified goals or standards), and (4)   the development and reporting of findings.

The most common and systematic procedure for accomplishing these tasks is presented in Figure III.2 and follows five steps (Hedstrom and Obbagy, 1988):

1.   *Identify and Understand Management Control Systems.*   This involves the identification and review of existing environmental control systems including planning, policies, communications, authority, record-keeping, monitoring administrative and physical controls. This is usually accomplished by literature reviews, interviews, questionnaires, and by direct observation. A facility tour and meeting with personnel to review the audit plan usually initiates the site visit process.

2.   *Assess Management Control Systems.*   The auditing team will assess management control systems to determine if lines of authority, responsibility, communications, and record- keeping are clearly defined, open, and functioning.

3.   *Gather Audit Evidence.*   Information on the environmental control system strengths and weaknesses are gathered by survey (questionnaires and checklists), interviews, observation, and testing (checking compliance records). All this information is gathered, recorded, and reported according to the audit plan or protocol.

4.   *Evaluate Audit Findings.*   Individual team-member findings are integrated and evaluated to list, prioritize and make certain adequate evidence has been acquired to assure accuracy of findings.

5.   *Report Findings to Facility Management.*   Informal discussions with personnel are held all during the audit process.

At the conclusion of the audit, a formal exist meeting is usually held with facility management to report and discuss important findings—in preparation for the production of formal draft and final reports. This provides the opportunity for management feedback prior to report production and ensures there are no surprises in the final report.

In addition to this process, the following elements are essential to insuring an audit is effective and yielding the maximum benefits (Hedstrom and Obbagy, 1988; ICC, 1988):

- Full Management Commitment—allocation of adequate authority, resources, and assurance of adequate follow-up of recommendations.
- Audit Team Objectivity
- Professional Competence—appropriate knowledge (e.g., environmental, technical, administrative, and legal) and experience (with similar companies or facilities)
- Well-Defined and Systematic Procedures—to assure comprehensive and sufficient coverage
- Clear and Appropriate Reporting—in specified formats sticking to factual, objective data, and observations
- Quality Assurance of the Auditing Procedure Over Time— to assure consistency and reliability
- Appropriate Follow-up—insure active implementation of recommendation.

*Issues.*   The issues most commonly profiled in an comprehensive environmental audit are summarized in Table III.2. The table is organized in categories of mass, energy, and information issues to correspond with policy categories recommended in Chapter II.

This list of audit issues is, by no means, all inclusive—individual firms with unique circumstances and problems will focus on differing menus of audited items. For example, management audits will focus on information issues; technical audits on manufacturing, pollution control, and energy technologies; and liability audits on pollution, wastes, safety and product hazards, and company compliance with legal requirements.

*Table III.2.* Issues Commonly Addressed in Comprehensive Environmental Audits

| MASS | INFORMATION |
|---|---|
| Pollution | Technology—Manufacturing, Pollution Control, and Energy |
| — air emissions | |
| — water emissions | — efficiency/and cost-effectiveness |
| Wastes | — safety |
| — solid wastes | — environmental impats |
| — hazardous wastes | — state-of-art |
| Resource | — reliability |
| — reduce | — self-sufficiency |
| — reuse | Management Controls |
| — recycle | — waste disposal |
| — hazardous materials | — on-site |
| Materials Storage | — off-site |
| — above ground | — communications |
| — below ground | — administrative authority/ |
| Site Assessments Facilities | responsibility |
| — asbestos | — capability |
| Products | — legal compliance |
| — durability | — emergency response |
| — hazardous materials | — fire |
| — safety | — spills |
| — testing quality controls | — medical/first aid |
| — recyclability | — recordkeeping |
| — biodegradability | Health and Safety Programs |
| Packaging | — employee-substance abuse, |
| — reuse, recycling | health and wellness program |
| — reduction | — occupational safety policies/ |
| Labeling/Information | procedures investigation, |
| | reporting medical surveillance |
| *ENERGY* | — transportation policies |
| | Recordkeeping/Reporting |
| Resources | Education |
| — sources/fuels | — job sefety occupational infor- |
| — amount | mation, training, and analysis |
| — cost | — personal health, safety, and |
| — end use | fitness |
| — availability | — management and investors |

(*continued*)

*Table III.2.* Continued

ITEMS TO BE ADDRESSED

| ENVIRONMENTAL | SAFETY | OCCUPATIONAL HEALTH | PRODUCT SAFETY |
| --- | --- | --- | --- |
| Site history | Safety policy/procedures | Employee exposure to air contaminants | Product safety program |
| Processes/materials | Accident reporting | Exposure to physical agents e.g. noise, radiation, heat etc. | Product quality control |
| Storage of materials above ground below ground | Accident recording | Measurements of employee exposure | Product packaging, storage and shipping |
| Air emissions | Accident investigation | Exposure records | Produce recall/withdrawal procedures |
| Water discharges | Permit to work systems | Ventilation/engineering controls | Customer information on product handling and quality |
| Solid wastes | Special procedures for: confined space entry work on electical equipment, breaking into pipe-lines, etc. | Personal portective equipment | Regulatory compliance |
| Liquid/hazardous wastes | Emergency response | Information and training on health hazards | Labeling |
| Asbestos | Fire fighting | Medical surveillance program | Specifications for purchased materials/products/packaging |
| Waste disposal on-site off-site | Job safety analysis | Hearing conservation | Material safety data |
| Oil/chemical spill prevention | Safety training | First aid | Vendor qualification program |
| Permits/licenses | Safety communication/ promotion | Regulatory requirements | QA testing and inspections |
|  | Housekeeping |  | Record keeping |
|  | Regulations compliance |  | Product literature |
|  |  |  | Process control |

*Source:* Baldwin (1991).

## Post-Audit Activities

Following the on-site audit, two important activities remain, the preparation of the final report and the development of a program of corrective or proactive action.

The preparation of the final report usually involves the preparation of a draft report, review, and comment by management for accuracy, and production of a final report by the team leader. These reports usually are presented in two parts (Maxwell, 1990):

- A formal statement of the company's current compliance with legal or corporate standards which includes an inventory and review of in-house programs—usually made available to the public.
- A summary of a program of future actions (which is usually kept private) to more fully comply with legal or company standards or to create or capture new business opportunities.

The preparation and implementation of plan and program of action to address problems or opportunities identified in the audit is usually the final and most important step in the audit process. This plan should be developed, approved, and implemented as quickly as possible. The action plan should be viewed by management as the culmination and ultimate goal of the audit process—rather than an afterthought following the collection of a lot of data. Procedures for monitoring progress (against specific goals or standards) should be developed and enforcement incentives and disincentives specified. A follow-up to assure the action plan is implemented may be done by the audit team, an internal team of experts, or by management (Hedstrom and Obbagy, 1988).

## AUDIT COSTS

Financial resources must be allocated to the audit process sufficient to design and implement the audit and to develop the action plan. While costs range widely according to the nature and scale of an environmental audit, general guidelines exist (Tusa, 1990). The design of a long-term replicable audit program will cost between

$10,000 and $100,000 and on-site audits usually cost about $2500 to $25,000 per site. A simple on-site audit may require only a few days for an experienced auditor with a simple set of question-naires—or may require a team of auditors as long as a week to do a comprehensive, detailed audit involving original research, checklists, or the development of a formal manual. In summary, the costs of designing and implementing an audit program are relatively small compared with the problems and costs associated with noncompliance and remediation. In addition, many direct economic benefits in the form of cost savings and new market opportunities are possible that could easily offset program costs.

## PITFALLS IN THE AUDITING PROCESS

From the perspective of loss control, implementation of an audit is problematic. This can be less if certain pitfalls are avoided in the auditing process (Tusa, 1990).

### Pre-Audit

- Inadequately defined corporate environmental policy can lead to a program that is inconsistent with the company's needs.
- The audit team may be missing credentials in key areas, resulting in inadequate audit coverage and depth of analysis.
- Plant personnel may not adequately implement pre-audit activities, resulting in inadequate resources and data collection and inappropriate audit procedures.

### Site-Audit

- Inadequate facility resources technical expertise.

### Post-Audit

- Lack of corporate commitment and/or resources can bring on more significant liabilities in the future, especially when recommendations are not acted on.

- A program that is not updated uses outmoded audit tools which also reduces the effectiveness of the audit and may even hurt the company's profitability in the long run.

## TRENDS IN AUDITING

As more companies recognize and accept that the environment is competitive, the number and nature of corporate environmental audits will increase. According to John Elkington, Director of SustainAbility Limited, one of the world's largest environmental consulting firms:

> Environmental auditing will not be a sufficient condition of business success in the 1990s, but increasingly it will be a necessary condition (*Business International*, 1990, p. 106).

Trends in environmental auditing fall into the general categories of (*Business International*, 1990; Hedstrom and Obbagy, 1988; and Priznar, 1990):

- Growth
- Diversification
- Globalization
- Standardization and professionalism
- Disclosure.

In the category of *growth*, the number of companies operating auditing programs is rapidly growing—with more and more small and intermediate-sized companies interested in the opportunities and efficiencies of an environmental audit. Further, company audit programs are *diversifying* from liability audits into programs covering products, raw materials, and employee health and safety. In addition to the expanding scope of audits, the narrowing of the focus of audits into specific categories of analysis based on identified problems and need will also provide opportunities for diversification and greater audit efficiency. Finally, the number and nature of audits are also increasing because of partnership requirements and acquisitions because of the need to reduce unforeseen liabilities.

The *globalization* of the environmental audit is also a significant recent trend with parent companies (with the "deepest pockets") concerned about liability and performance of overseas facilities, subsidiaries, partners, vendors, and suppliers. Subsidiaries with more stringent environmental reporting and management requirements (e.g., in Europe) are pushing parent companies to develop company-wide audit and management programs.

Perhaps the most significant trend in the future is the *standardization and professionalization* of the environmental audit. The growth in auditing will foster better techniques, procedures, and reporting of the results of environmental audits to promote quality control and replication.

Pressure from government, industrial associations (trying to improve image) and citizen, community, and environmental groups will lead to increased disclosure of audit results. In several countries (e.g., Hong Kong, the United Kingdom, Sweden, Denmark, and Norway) governments are developing programs to "encourage" companies to perform audits with the possibility that the audit programs would become compulsory sometime in the future (with more standardized techniques procedures and reporting requirements) (*Business International*, 1990).

In summary, care in team selection, provision of adequate resources, and careful attention to detail and procedure, as described in this paper, can and has produced considerable benefit to companies by reducing liabilities, improving efficiency and capturing new markets. By accomplishing an audit, companies can, in essence, "do well by doing good."

## Chapter IV

# *The Evolution and Development of Environmental Auditing*

As corporations invest more in environmental auditing, a number of issues have arisen, including how audits should be performed, who should conduct audits, and what skills are necessary to complete audits. Debate over whether to employ internal versus external auditors, whether audits should be called something else (e.g., evaluations), and what standards should guide professional practice also is present. Clearly, because the practice of environmental evaluation has evolved from the preparation of environmental impact statements to comprehensive evaluations of corporate performance, a number of issues relating to approach and methodology have arisen.

The Environmental Protection Agency (EPA) definition of "environmental auditing" is used herein as a benchmark (Priznar, 1990). EPA's definition of environmental auditing is elegantly simple and widely accepted. "Environmental auditing is a systematic, documented, periodic and objective review by regulated entities of facility operations and practices related to meeting environmental requirements." This definition is broad enough to include inspections, assessments, surveys, and evaluations. Regardless of the significant differences among these activities, the trends presented still apply. The demand for efficiency, control, and quality has forced a dramatic shift toward automated information systems in auditing. Automation is crucial to enhanced productivity and quality improvement because there are too many federal, state, and local regulations to track and understand, vastly different facilities to evaluate, too many audits to conduct, and not enough good and experienced auditors. Automated tools are now available to assist auditors. While new hardware and software programs appear in a steady stream, the best automated auditing aid should have three fundamental features: an easily searched regulatory citation text system, a word processing capability permitting quick report development, and a database developed to track and sort findings to facilitate ad hoc reporting needs.

An automated full-text regulation retrieval system makes it more convenient to search for applicable regulations in a given situation. Specifically, searching for key words (e.g., training, PCBs) finds relevant citations more efficiently and completely than a manual search.

In terms of developing audit reports, word processing automation again is beneficial as a time-saver. Many series or specialty audit reports are boilerplate, with spaces to insert variables such as site-specific information and findings. With the format and outline already established, the auditor needs to key in only technical data. This promotes standardization, completeness, and efficiency.

Too often, great volumes of audit data are compiled without planning for analysis and use. One organization, for example, completed dozens of facility audits before deciding to prepare a summary report. That decision resulted in a painful and time-consuming process of revisiting all the reports and reinterpreting, classifying, and categorizing thousands of findings. All this could have been avoided with sensible planning. Because it is not always possible to know how audit data will be used, a flexible database management system is critically important. It can provide the versatility needed to quickly produce a variety of ad hoc reports, benefiting just about any type of organization.

Many auditors travel from one facility to another. The best audit reports are developed as soon as possible. If a report is not prepared during an audit, shortly thereafter, or at least before the next one begins, there will always be some critical memory loss and sense of urgency in recording findings. To prevent this, many auditors now take laptop computers and portable printers on site. This way, they can leave a draft report on disk with the client or send a disk to the office to have a hardcopy draft report reviewed and waiting for them on their return.

Automated auditing produces at least three predictable results: improved computer skills among auditors, continued development of auditing automation tools, and increased utilization of audit data. Of these three, the last result is the most important because it will have the largest impact on corporations and government agencies. Environmental auditing has been likened to a management information system because it provides management with specific information on how an organization is performing with respect to environmental compliance requirements. When linked with other corporate information systems, environmental audit data will reach its full potential by assuring compliance and aiding financial planning, new product lines and expansions, and generally risk management.

One large company, for example, modified its internal information systems so that audit findings can be integrated with other related corporate databases. These include environmental compliance tracking systems and systems traditionally used to manage business, such as operating budgets, facility improvement plans, personnel performance monitoring and planning, health and safety program monitoring and planning, health and safety program monitoring, and production activity scheduling. Integrated databases make it easier for managers to understand and react to audit findings because they can be causally linked to a wider range of activities or staff. Additionally, integrated databases improve compliance management by helping managers understand relationships among a wider range of variables, giving them more options for mitigating problems. This will eventually result in more effective compliance management.

The ethical and moral questions surrounding disclosure of audit findings are a growing concern among auditors and their employers. It is sufficient to inform only the auditor's direct supervisor or client when an auditor discovers practices or records at a facility that indicate serious, willful noncompliance, especially practices that seem likely to result in harm to human health? Put another way, should the auditor, upon learning of or even strongly suspecting a situation with significant threat to human health or the environment, directly inform regulatory authorities? There is no one right answer to this question. However, recent work on this subject has helped clarify the issue pointing out that the legal and ethical implications of the disclosure issue may not necessarily dictate the same course of action. Guidelines to resolve this potential conflict should be promulgated in corporate policy, in professional codes of ethics, and in environmental regulations themselves. This "ethics" contention will continue to occur absent a move toward more corporate awareness and the professionalization of environmental auditing.

Legal techniques, such as creating an attorney-client privilege or attorney work product, can be used to help ensure the confidentiality of audit information, but there is uncertainty whether absolute protection exists. For example, EPA may request audit reports on a case-by-case basis. While these legal techniques may provide some control, they all depend on a commitment by the participants to maintain an information control strategy. The issue typically becomes the willingness to participate in the face of internal ethical pressures.

Obviously much depends on the auditor's personal beliefs, values, and responsibilities and relationship to the employer, but there are some legal obligations and requirements that can alter the auditor's decision on how to proceed when confronted with an ethical concern. It is clear, for example, that if an auditor discovers a chemical spill exceeding the reportable quantity, he or she must ensure that response authorities are contacted within 24 hours. While the regulatory requirement should relieve any ethical question, it is surprising how employees' fears of being transferred or terminated for disclosure impact their choosing the correct courses of action.

Auditors must also make decisions about unascertainable issues that involve uncertainty as to the nature and extent of a problem due to a lack of sufficient technology or legal data. This area is murky and creates most of the concern and debate among auditors. Many good auditors are driven by a feeling that they are doing something important and "right." Moreover, to maintain their enthusiasm and tenacity, they must see results from their efforts. Making the same finding time after time is one of the most discouraging things that an auditor encounters. If considered serious enough, it can become very difficult for some auditors not to make an anonymous phone call to a regulatory agency. The potential for these uncontrolled information releases may drive large firms to conduct audits using their own teams of employees rather than consultants.

There are other options available to management to help reduce the risk of uncontrolled information releases. These may seem fundamental, nonresponsive, or unhelpful, but they still present alternatives that are used by some firms. One option is not to have audits conducted. This may seem ridiculous, since managers must understand their facility's condition in order to make good business decisions. Nevertheless, the axiom "Don't ask the question if you don't want to hear the answer" holds especially true in this case. Some managers feel they cannot afford to learn of additional demands to which they cannot respond. Another alternative is to treat auditors and their information very seriously. The number of times a frustrated or disillusioned employee caused problems for a current or previous employer is incalculable. If this disgruntled employee is or was an auditor, the potential for problems through uncontrolled information release is enormous. Finally, auditors should agree to a tight reporting hierarchy before they begin an assignment. This way, everyone involved will know who gets the information and when. This is in a sense a screening process. Auditors who cannot agree to a corporate reporting sequence and hierarchy pose a risk to the facility by possibly releasing information.

Several outcomes are likely as a result of these ethical issues in environmental auditing. When corporate management and counsel take measures designed to maximize a legal shield around audit findings, increasing care will be given to choosing the staff involved as well as the process for controlling information. Corporate proactivity in environmental program management will be triggered by managers who have been exposed to or have experienced these ethical problems and understand the corporation's compliance policies, supervisory responsibilities, and liabilities. Finally, ethics will promote professionalization.

Environmental auditing's status as a profession is controversial. The field is still so new and there are so many variables that many knowledgeable people do not believe environmental auditing is really a profession. Nevertheless, the future of environmental auditing seems clear—it must ultimately be standardized and supported by a formal professionalization program.

The professionalizing of environmental auditing is driven by several forces, including ethics, professional development, peer recognition, regulatory initiatives, and information transfer. However, aside from a few articles, there is surprisingly little written about this movement. A number of organizations have studied environmental auditor professionalization. The first formal organization for auditing, the Institute for Environmental Auditing, has hosted a series of meetings on the subject. Another organization, the Environmental Auditing Roundtable, has a committee studying auditor credentials. A third group, the Environmental Forum, is strongly interested in the issue but has not pursued professionalization as a key agenda item. These groups have made some progress, but there is no clear resolution for the issues impeding professionalization, such as deciding who is qualified, what standards should be developed, and who or what organization can sanction auditors.

Many environmental auditors feel the need for professionalization. This is evidenced by their eager willingness to pay for registration or participate in certifying organizations. These efforts, while giving recognition to auditing professionals with some qualifications, add little real value to the individual professionally. Thousands of individuals annually pay dues to be affiliated with one or more of the new certifying or registering organization, despite the fact that as yet there is no meaningful registration or certification program for environmental auditors. One potential exception is the voluntary environmental assessor registration program sponsored by the California Environmental Affairs Agency, which was created by the Environmental Quality Assessment Act of 1986. It is still too soon to tell how effective that program will be. Key issues need to be resolved, such as its real value to auditors, acceptance by practitioners, and reciprocity with other potential state programs.

Until an accepted professionalization program is in place, there is uncertain value to current environmental auditing affiliations. Certainly if one participates in an auditor organization it indicates a willingness or interest in improving or maintaining skills, but at this time affiliation does not necessarily imply quality.

The need for professionalization is clear. Regardless of differences in name, end use, and scope, the practices included in environmental auditing have fundamental similarities. The areas of common ground could be the basis for initiating professional standards. Without this endorsement, the standards will always be suspect.

The probable outcome is that there will ultimately be an environmental auditor profession. There will be professional standards and possibly a government-sanctioned regulatory structure. It is only a matter of time until someone or an organization takes the lead and does a credible job of pulling interested parties together. It is critical, however, that auditors avoid the development of a negative image caused by unqualified practitioners conducting faulty audits and costing clients huge sums of money. Professionalization will reduce the risk. Few, if any, countries are as advanced as the United States in environmental auditing. This creates problems for some and opportunities for many. Interest in environmental auditing as a management tool at an international level has existed for some time. With broad support, the International Chamber of Commerce (ICC) prepared and published a position paper on environmental auditing last June. In doing this, the ICC asserted a leadership position that will probably shape the direction of international environmental auditing. The policy statement is consistent with the expectations and practices of most auditors in the United States.

Many large U.S.-based corporations have overseas operations subject to foreign regulations and customs that are not necessarily similar to foreign regulations and customs that are not necessarily similar to those followed in the United States. In many cases, a U.S.-based company must decide if it will apply more stringent U.S. requirements. Since many of these facilities are located overseas because of economic criteria, including a more relaxed set of environmental standards, there is often a conflict of interests. In these situations, auditors must decide which standards to apply in the overseas audits—U.S. standards or less stringent local requirements.

There are strong and differing opinions on this fundamental question that present conflicts between environmental ethics and economics. Do corporations want to know that their operations overseas do not meet the same standards worldwide? It is hard to rationalize choosing between environmental ethics and economics, especially with standards affecting human health. Fortunately, many U.S.-based corporations are acting responsibly in this regard. There are, however, numerous problems in implementing U.S. standards overseas, such as differences in culture, communication problems, differences in regulations or a lack of them, differences in enforcement, difficulty in finding trained staff, politically sensitive situations or instability, corporate relationships (e.g., partial ownership) with local governments.

There also can be significant problems with foreign-based corporations that have acquired or opened facilities in the United States. When these transactions occur, the owners must be made aware of the importance of environmental laws. They could learn too late that they own a hazardous waste site or a facility with huge fines levied against it for poor environmental practices. In these cases, the cost of business can jump dramatically.

A good example of where environmental auditing can help occurred recently. A large European-based conglomerate prepared for months to purchase a specialty chemical manufacturer in the United States. Initially, the conglomerate suspected no environmental regulatory difficulties, since the feedstocks and products were widely accepted and loosely regulated. Just days before the deal was to be made, the conglomerate decided to audit for environmental concerns. Checking with EPA revealed proposed regulations that would affect the target firm's profitability and operating plan. In particular, there was a good chance that the target's products would be environmentally unacceptable in nearly all current applications. The deal was called off.

The internationalization of corporations have qualified staff to conduct environmental audits, they are rarely distributed evenly among overseas facilities. Local consultants may be preferred because of such advantages as understanding local language, customs, and regulations, and their ability to fully functioning and available of short notice.

Environmental auditing will likely be one of the pioneering tools used to stimulate standardization in worldwide environmental management and practices. Globalization of environmental auditing will also promote good corporate citizenship and accountability. There will be explosive growth in environmental auditing opportunities worldwide.

Diversification is broadening the scope of environmental auditing and narrowing the focus of specialty audits. By broadening in scope, environmental auditing is evolving into a tool that can be used for total risk management. Two examples illustrate this point. First, many organizations are including health and safety concerns in environmental audits. Environmental auditors, practicing for many years, almost all agree that they felt their work was incomplete when a full audit centered only on the traditional environmental concerns, such as air pollution, and waste management. Consequently, it is not unreasonable for what is known as a health and safety survey to be included in an environmental audit.

Second, even though the body of environmental laws and regulations is large, there are numerous practices and situations apparent to an experienced auditor that present environmental risks that are not regulated. In fact, regulatory compliance is no guarantee against liability. Thus, an audit that includes an identification of risks beyond compliance is a reasonable extension of the audit's scope.

Environmental auditing can also be narrow in scope. For example, specialty audits have been recognized for some time and include waste minimization audits, third-party liability audits, audits for real estate transactions, and management effectiveness audits. As subsets of full audits, these specialty audits focus on understanding only a portion of what ordinarily constitutes a full program audit. Some of these specialty audits have become so customized for a specific objective or client type that unique terms and conditions for performing the work are spreading nationally. For example, in auditing property transfers it is now important to understand that there are commonly three audit phases offered. (Phase II and Phase III audits are in most cases not really audits, but the nomenclature is gaining acceptance.)

Federal environmental laws, such as the Resource conservation and Recovery Act (RCRA) and the Emergency Preparedness and Community Right-to-Know Act (EPCRA) have spurred audit diversification, or specialty audits. Even more specifically, New Jersey's Environmental Cleanup and Responsibility Act requires "that any place of business where hazardous materials were stored or handled in any way be given a clean bill of health by the state before a transfer of ownership or change of operation takes place." The result of this statute has been an increase in the number of consulting environmental auditors. These auditors then complete property evaluations for their clients who in turn must submit them to the state.

While these audits have become extremely specialized, the need for diversified audits continues to grow. Some of the factors in favor of diversification audits continue to grow. Some of the factors in favor of diversification include the need for risk and liability management, insurance information requirements, and budgetary planning. These factors create special audit objectives and auditing techniques, but can easily be incorporated into a general environmental audit.

The flexibility of the traditional environmental audit allows auditors to focus or expand their product for a special need or client. These specialty audits have arisen primarily because of regulatory requirements and will continue to evolve to fit unique market or program niches.

The main criteria for auditor selection, in the absence of accepted standards and a code of ethics, is an auditor's specialized experience and cost. Some consulting firms have focused on the most active auditing market segments, such as real estate transactions. The result is an "assembly-line" audit that only covers the most rudimentary and obvious problems, such as compliance status. Lack of knowledge often causes buyers to use price as the primary, if not sole, factor in selecting an auditor even though the lowest cost is not necessarily the best value. "Caveat emptor," usually mentioned in reference to the purchase of real property, applies to environmental services as well.

Most external auditors come from a consulting firm, which raises a market practice that buyers need to be aware of. This is the old "foot in the door" routine. Some consulting firms offer audits at low cost to establish a client relationship. If their auditor learns of more serious problems while performing the audit, the consulting firm may position itself to gain more lucrative follow-up work. Not all consulting firms do this, but many do and admit it freely to their colleagues as a successful marketing technique. There is nothing wrong with offering add-on services to clients who are in need, but searching for lucrative problems to solve, consultants can lose sight of their primary mission to do a thorough audit.

There is a simple, sensible method for classifying and subsequently choosing external auditors. It relies on matching needs with knowledge and skill levels. There are important differences among auditors' knowledge and skill levels and this has a substantial impact on audits. First, evaluate and understand auditing needs. Is a focused or limited audit sufficient? The better the need is understood, the better will be the decision to choose the external auditor. As an example, a large international consulting firm is probably best qualified to audit the effectiveness of worldwide environmental program operations for an international firm or government organization. Alternately, to effectively audit the compliance status of commercial real estate in New Jersey, the best firm would be the one closest to the property with a good track record in that particular type of audit. These differences are dramatic but they make an important point. Each company and each auditor has its own style and strengths. These should be matched with a client's needs and specific facilities to ensure the audit is meaningful.

# Part II

## REGULATION AND CORPORATE ENVIRONMENTALISM

# Chapter V

# *Environmental and Other Regulation to Compensate for Externalities*

A considerable amount of government regulation is based on the economic theory of externalities. Positive and negative externalities, also called spillovers or external economies and diseconomies, may be defined as the consequences of events of exchanges that are not automatically compensated for in market prices. In the case of negative externalities the parties to an economic transaction or set of transactions do not bear the full costs of their actions. Some costs, the external costs, are borne by third parties, whose interests are not reflected in the market signals that attract participants to the transaction. Left alone, some parties will produce too much of a commodity, such as toxic particles emitted into the air, from the view of the general populace. Production, distribution, and/or consumption may produce costs that are overlooked by the market. The typical example of consumption externalities is the tragedy of the commons. In this example, grazers of sheep on common lands collectively destroy the productive capacity of the land trying to feed their sheep. From this perspective the enclosure movement of the fourteenth and fifteenth centuries may be thought of as an early and highly successful form of successful government intervention on behalf of the environment.

In the case of positive externalities, or external benefits, the reverse is true. Because parties to a transaction cannot appropriate all the benefits that result from it, they will ignore the benefits that accrue to third parties in making their spending decisions. From the view of society as a whole, the result will be that too few externality-producing transactions will occur.

Government regulates and provides subsidies to stimulate the output of some commodities that are thought to have external economies associated with their production. For example, regulatory policy and tax subsidies encourage innovative investments by industry and support public and private education. In the case of education, there are elements of direct regulation by government related to social welfare and service quality in that parents are required to send their children to school. Also, education service distribution is regulated professionally, geographically, and in other ways. An important case of government regulation to support the production of externality-creating outputs is the complex of regulations to protect intellectual property. Without copyright, patent, and related laws, it is generally believed that the supply of new ideas in industry and in the cultural sphere would be severely curtailed. Government regulation attempts to remedy market failure in production and distribution of intellectual goods and services that would otherwise limit production of these externality-creating outputs. Market failure in this instance is a result of the fact that preventing distribution of intellectual products to other than paying customers is not feasible without regulation.

Attempts to compensate for externalities encompass a wide range of government regulatory activity, and one that has increased in scope in recent years. In particular, environmental quality regulation has expanded rapidly. Until the environmental pollution resulting from industrialization, rapid technological changes, and other factors became impossible to ignore, the assimilative capabilities of the air, water, and land were treated essentially as free goods. This was natural enough because producers and consumers of any particular commodity generally bore only a tiny fraction of the environmental costs associated with its production and use. Recognition of the dangers inherent in a laissez-faire policy has led inevitably to regulation to limit or prohibit environmental degradation. Environmental protection regulation is embodied in legislation such as the Clean Air Act and rules promulgated by regulatory agencies on the authority of legislative mandates.

Environmental regulation seeks to reduce harmful emissions by directly prohibiting them, by mandating reductions in emissions to a specified level (performance standards), or by requiring some corrective action (engineering standards, for example, requiring all new stationary sources to employ a specified but available emissions reduction technology). Because there is no doubt that air, water, and other types of pollution can cause demonstrable damage to public health and tend to reduce the quality of life, that environmental regulation produces real economic benefits is beyond question.[1] The problem with environmental regulation is that it is far from costless. In addition to the decision-making, monitoring, and enforcement costs associated with antitrust policy or direct regulation, not to mention the more subtle x-inefficiency losses, there are losses associated with regulation-induced politicization of an industry. This form of government action can and does impose huge compliance costs on both firms and consumers. Of course, to an extent these costs are justified and unavoidable. The question is: To what extent? We should want to be sure that the benefits of environmental regulation exceed their costs and that emissions reductions are achieved at the lowest possible costs.

Unfortunately, owing to the incredible complexity of environmental regulations, it is not possible to uncategorically conclude that the benefits they produce are sufficient to justify the costs they impose on industry and on the economy in general. Indeed, any meaningful answer to this question must be highly disaggregated: Is a particular emissions-reducing technology efficient when mandated for a specific firm or plant, in a particular area, from the standpoint of a target pollutant: Nevertheless, ambitious attempts to overcome the formidable measurement and other methodological problems involved in evaluating the benefits and costs of environmental protection have been made in recent years. One example is the U.S. Environmental Protection Agency's analysis of the costs and benefits of compliance with the Clean Air Amendments of 1970. This study made numerous assumptions about how industries, governments, and consumers would respond to the ambient standards and timetables set by the law. The procedures and methodologies used in this analysis are instructive, if somewhat dated. The EPA found that the benefits of meeting the Clean Air Act standards exceeded the cost of compliance by several billion dollars (constant 1970 dollars). Henry M. Peskin and several colleagues reanalyzed the EPA data after making various adjustments and filling in some information gaps (one large data gap was the neglect of benefits resulting from auto emission controls by EPA; in addition, many EPA cost figures have to be revised upward) (Peskin and Seskin, 1975). They found that estimated costs exceeded estimated benefits by about $20 billion. The research also divided that data by industry, finding substantial differences in the balance between costs and benefits across various industries. This suggested that air pollution control efforts, at least of the type the EPA envisioned at that time, would be far more cost-beneficial to some industries than to others.

In contrast with these results, after 10 years of study of the research on the relationship between air pollution and human health, Lave and Seskin (1977) concluded that if EPA estimates of the costs of cutting particulate and sulfur oxide emissions from stationary sources to mandated levels were correct, realized benefits of such controls from reduced mortality alone would likely exceed total costs by some 70% annually. However, the same study also concluded that, at the margin, the benefits of achieving current mandated standards for mobile sources of air pollution were less than the costs. This analysis suggested that a "two car" strategy—emphasizing strict standards and enforcement where pollution damages are worst—would achieve most of the benefits of a more uniform national program but would reduce costs measurably. Indeed, most empirical analyses of the benefits and costs of environmental regulation agree on one point: When the objective of public policy is a reduction in emissions of a target pollutant, uniform standards (e.g., mandating a uniform percentage reduction in emissions or the use of a single abatement technology) will not achieve an efficient result. In many cases, uniform standards imply compliance costs 6 to 10 times greater than the minimum required to reduce total emissions to some target level.[2]

Recognition of these problems has led to reconsideration of previously rejected alternatives to regulation. In fact, economists have for some time argued that the most efficient institutional arrangement for reducing harmful emissions or other damage-producing externalities is an economic sanction or tax levied on residual emissions and set to equal the damage caused by increments to pollutant concentrations. Under this proposal, decisions as to where and how to reduce emissions levels would be explicitly delegated to firms. Damages or, if damage measurement presented insuperable problems, residual emissions would be continuously monitored and penalties would be directly proportional to emissions levels. Many economists argue that such a levy would minimize the cost, reducing total emissions to a target level.[3] In theory, an emissions tax would bring the polluter's cost-benefit calculus in line with society, and polluters would have, therefore, an incentive to invest in pollution abatement equipment up to the point where the costs and benefits of abatement are equal. Consequently, an emissions tax would "lead some to reduce pollution to a greater extent, some to a lesser extent, depending on the marginal benefits of polluting in each case" (Fisher and Peterson, 1978). European examples (see Kneese, 1975) and an extensive body of theoretical analysis (Atkinson and Lewis, 1974, pp. 237-250; Chapman, 1974; Griffin, 1974) indicate that such an institutional arrangement could be extremely cost-effective in reducing emissions.

This approach was carried one step further by Dales (1968), who argues that because the market failure here arises as a consequence of the absence of a market in the assimilative capacity of the environment, the solution is to create a market wherein rights or purchasable permits to pollute may be bartered among polluting firms. Under Dales's scheme, a pollution control agency would establish concentration standards for a region. It would then auction off the rights to contribute to pollution concentrations to the highest bidders. According to Fisher and Peterson: "[I]f the costs and benefits of pollution, or pollution abatement, are known to the control board, the pollution rights market can lead to the same (efficient) level of pollution as a tax" (Fisher and Peterson, 1978).

Dales's program has never been tried as proposed. Nevertheless, there are pollution rights markets throughout the United States. In these instances, the EPA has established regional nondegradation standards. Firms are expressly prohibited from adding to pollution concentrations except where they can secure an equivalent reduction in emissions elsewhere within the region. However, subject to other EPA standards (standby controls that are required to respond to changing weather patterns, and so on), they are granted the right to continue to generate emissions at existing levels or to transfer those rights to other firms in the region. With the help of state officials who have created inventories of these assets, this has led to the creation of active markets in pollution rights (or offsets). Where pollution concentrations approach optimal levels, this seems to be a nearly ideal solution to the problem: It is straightforward, easily enforcable, and controlled by means of environmental impact statements. Furthermore, once such a market is established, it could facilitate the efficient transition to lower concentration levels in areas where concentrations of harmful emissions are excessive. In this case, all firms would be required to make uniform cutbacks in emission levels of a given amount (e.g., 5% a year) or arrange for equivalent reductions elsewhere in the zone. Public intervention could facilitate the operation of such a market and would probably be necessary to police it. However, once established, market forces should be sufficient to ensure that the total reduction in emissions sought would be obtained at least cost.[4] We may also note that the marketable rights approach can be applied in other areas to allocate scarce resources: airport landing and takeoff spaces, hospital services (beds or equipment), the electromagnetic spectrum (radio frequencies) (U.S. Regulatory Council, 1980).

Under the Carter administration and to some extent through the efforts of the U.S. Regulatory Council (terminated by Reagan in 1981), and more recently since 1988, marketable rights and other innovative and market-oriented approaches to regulation have been given greater consideration and use in regulatory policy. In addition, economists have looked more closely at the very real problems of information availability and cost, uncertainty, and administrative feasibility that present obstacles to the implementation of market-oriented regulatory approaches. Similar review of the effectiveness of emissions taxation schemes was undertaken and has been heeded by U.S. federal and state government regulators and policy makers in recent years (Tietenberg, 1973).

The proximate goal of pollution control is the reduction of pollutant concentrations, not simply the reduction of emissions. In some cases, the effect of a reduction in emissions will be a corresponding reduction in pollution concentration. But this appears to be a rather special case. Generally, owing to the environment's capacity to assimilate certain pollutants, variations in meteorological conditions, proximity to populations at risk, and so forth, an individual firm's contribution to concentrations, let alone its contribution to hazard levels, cannot be assured to be directly proportional to its total emissions of harmful residues.

This implies that if a tax scheme were adopted, it would have to be modified frequently to maintain environmental quality. Consequently, a better strategy would likely include a mix of taxes and standards. However, under a marketable permits scheme, a reasonably satisfactory solution might be to assign permits so as to reflect plant locations and meteorological conditions. For example, various classes of marketable permits are issued that are good only under conditions specified by local air quality managers, as in Table V.1. Unfortunately, the more complex the permit process, the more costly are the monitoring and enforcement costs.

Many market- or performance-oriented institutional arrangements require continuous monitoring of emissions at the plant level, which is far more costly than is inspection of equipment or procedures. Furthermore, monitoring costs make no direct contribution to emissions reductions. In some cases, it may be that firms' personnel will be less competent to determine how best to meet emissions standards than are their counterparts in regulatory agencies. Finally, the fact of the matter is that we do not really know how responsive firms are to incentives, or how much a given tax would reduce emissions levels. Nor do we know how to design and manage a full-fledged market in pollution permits. The fact is that much of the discussion surrounding these alternative institutional arrangements is highly speculative (this is also true of regulation as well). While we believe these mechanisms have considerable potential, realization of that potential will be delayed until such time as the factual information upon which more effective policies can be based in provided. The best way to get this kind of information is through a systematic program of experimentation.

*Table V.1.   Classes of Marketable Air Quality Permits*

| Permit Class | Authorization |
|---|---|
| 1 | Good under all weather conditions |
| 2 | Good except during stage 3 alerts |
| 3 | Good except during stages 2 and 3 alerts |
| 4 | Good except during stages 1, 2, and 3 alerts |
| 5 | Good only when weather conditions are most favorable |

One other compelling institutional arrangement should also be mentioned here; this alternative emphasizes the influence of market incentives through tax expenditure rather than regulatory policy. Tax expenditures (tax revenues foregone by government) provide reductions in the taxes owed by business and industry in order to provide capital for investment in pollution abatement. In essence, use of tax expenditures to improve environmental quality depends on establishment of contracts between government and private firms to the effect that money left in the private sector will be used to meet quality objectives embodied in regulation. However, the effectiveness of this approach is dependent on the extent to which standards are met. This remains even though regulatory control is relaxed.

This is particularly evident under the tax expenditure policy changes enacted into law under the Reagan administration. These changes enabled industry to buy and sell tax credits provided by government to satisfy a variety of objectives, including environmental quality. Creation of a market for tax credits implies even further that government must monitor the outcomes of tax expenditure policy so that private sector obligations to invest in pollution abatement technology, purchased by government though tax expenditures, actually result in desired improvements in performance. If the exchange of tax credits blurs responsibility for investment is the most efficient means for maintaining or improving environmental quality, then the objectives sought by tax expenditures as an alternative to direct regulatory control will not have been met. This would tend to support advocates of direct regulation, at the expense of tax expenditure policy. From a theoretical economic perspective, there are strong reasons to believe that a tax expenditure market will result in improved performance in the long run. Still, as we observe in so many areas of regulation, theory often does not encompass complexities of application that, in some instances, are significant enough to make theory invalid.

At present, there is little consensus on environmental quality taxation approaches, despite acknowledgment of their attractiveness as general alternatives to direct control through regulation. The need to define and resolve problems of information, uncertainty, instrument and institutional design, and others remains. Some of these problems are addressed subsequently in this paper. In the meantime it makes sense to us to apply the net-benefit criterion (benefits minus costs) to help determine how policy should be set. This assumes the possibility of a shifting public consensus on the levels of acceptable environmental quality, without specifying the direction of the shirt.

The environmental quality problem is by no means the only case of government regulation to deal with negative externalities. As noted, another important class of cases involves instances of depletable resources. When business and industry, groups of consumers, or a society depend on a common but exhaustible resource, market signals may not fully reflect the true value of the resource. Prices will reflect costs of production that may change as the resource is depleted, plus demand pressure, and other factors. But they will not be influenced automatically by the fact that exhaustion of the resource will cause economic and social dislocation. As discussed earlier under the tragedy of the commons example, in situations where the market price as a consequence is too low, government must intervene to ration the resource or to prohibit further depletion. Rationing may be accomplished through definition of legal rights to the resource and regulation schedules reflecting the relative priorities of various consumers, through prices or other means.

Another area in which government intervenes through regulation to stimulate production is in markets for information. In many cases firms have no incentive to provide information about product hazards, workplace safety, or aspects of their operations that may be sufficiently valuable to consumers or workers to justify the costs of provision. In some cases, government requires the provision of additional information beyond what would be supplied by the unregulated market. The next section addresses the costs and benefits of information provision and alternative regulatory strategies in such situations.

## REGULATION TO COMPENSATE FOR IMPERFECTIONS IN MARKETS FOR INFORMATION

Among the assumptions that must be met if unfettered market arrangements are to produce the most efficient allocation of society's resources is the assumption that economic agents (producers, consumers, workers) have sufficient information about the costs and benefits of their alternative choices to make rational decisions. Alas, there are a wide range of situations where decisions must be made with very imperfect information, due to the fact that relevant information is either very costly or impossible to obtain.

The rationale for a considerable portion of environmental, health, and safety regulation is that unregulated market arrangements will not produce optimal levels of the information that economic agents need in their decision making. Consequently, prices, wages, product consumption levels, injury and accident rates, and so on will be different and less satisfactory than they would be if information were adequate. Producer firms, even if they possess such information, have little incentive to provide information to consumers that may reduce product sales or to provide information to workers about job hazards that may result in the need to pay higher wages or to make costly changes to reduce hazards. For that matter, they may have little incentive to obtain such information in the first place. Consequently, workers and consumers are often unable to obtain relevant information and may be unable to utilize it properly even if they do get it, often because it is difficult for the layperson to interpret. Our point is that, because information is not a purely private good, efficient quantities of it are unlikely to be produced by private entrepreneurs (see Davis and Kamien, 1970). Thus, there is an economic as well as a political rationale for government intervention in such areas as product and worker safety.

Government interventions in response to failures in information markets fall into several broad categories, based on the reasons for the shortages of usable information. In circumstances where consumers, workers, or others could presumably utilize information properly if it were available, and where the information in question can be developed at a cost that does not appear to exceed the expected benefits from its development, governments employ strategies that depend on individual economic actors to utilize information. Government may, for example, conduct or sponsor research on the nature, incidence, and prevention of product or workplace hazards and disseminate this information free or at subsidized prices to potential users. The Consumer Product Safety Commission and the Occupational Safety and Health Administration (through the National Institute for Occupational Safety and Health) support millions of dollars worth of information-gathering and disseminating activities each year.

Another approach, sometimes integrated with the first, is to require firms to collect and provide information about product or job hazards to consumers and workers. Consumers and workers may then use the information, along with data about prices, wages, and other relevant characteristics, to satisfy their preferences more efficiently than would be possible in the absence of the information.

A third approach is to structure economic incentives so as to ensure that costs associated with product and workplace hazards will be taken into account in economic decisions. Business and industry then have an incentive to develop the appropriate amount of information to utilize their costs, for example, about causes and preventions of occupational injuries or product-related accidents. When the hazard is limited entirely to parties to private market transactions, such an incentive may be created by making one party (usually the employer or the seller, as he is assumed to be the better-informed party as to the level of hazard) responsible for compensating the other for damages incurred as a consequence of the transaction. This may be accomplished indirectly, via a body of tort law (by making it possible for the damaged party to sue for compensation on a case-by-case basis), through some form of no-fault compensation scheme (such as workers' compensation), or by some combination of the two. Also, it may be done by imposing a public tax on adverse health consequences and public compensation of the injured party.

Problems of environmental, worker and product health and safety have been traditionally addressed through such mechanisms. But in their design and development, little attention has been given to the part they might play in providing firms with an incentive to reduce hazards. Instead, income maintenance and post hoc compensation have been emphasized. This may have unnecessarily reduced the effectiveness of these mechanisms as a means of promoting efficient hazard reduction decisions.

For example, workers' compensation laws shift much of the liability of workplace exposure and accidents to employers. Employers are required to carry insurance to pay off claims that may arise under the program. In turn, the premium an employer pays is based on his firm's accident record. This provides an incentive for reducing hazards. However, under most workers' compensation laws, there is a fixed upper limit on the amount that can be paid to any given claimant. Thus, hazards that have low probabilities of causing severe damages are likely to be underprevented under such a scheme. On the other hand, overemphasis is likely given to preventing hazards that result in frequent but minor losses. Finally, firms are frequently made liable for outcomes over which they have no control, for example, injuries that occur on the way to the workplace. However, it is one thing to say that it is inappropriate to address problems of income maintenance by means of workers' compensation (to do so distorts the proper purpose of these programs), and quite another to say how this objective ought to be pursued.

It should also be noted that the system of tort liability compensates, to a degree, for the limits placed on workers' compensation. If the firm can be shown to be negligent, the injured party may successfully sue for compensation. However, it is no simple matter to prove negligence. Moreover, litigation is costly and time consuming, and the existing liability system limits compensation in several ways, for example, a firm's maximum liability is its net worth. This may be one explanation for the frequently observed phenomenon that large firms comply with regulations more readily than do small firms. Consequently, except where events with certain causes are concerned and where the damages inflicted do not push against institutionalized limits to compensation, we cannot expect the possibility of legal action to be 100% efficient in leading firms to invest in preventing accidents or sickness. Furthermore, there is reason to believe that the tort systems may not ensure equitable compensation for injured parties.

The point of this discussion is that an economist would likely reverse the targets of employer liability and workers' compensation and provide for income maintenance by some wholly independent means. Legal accountability should be most effective where it is addressed to known hazards with known consequences—to situations where negligence is fairly easily demonstrated. Workers' compensation, on the other hand, should be targeted at open-ended losses, which result from partially indeterminate causes, and shared responsibility for hazards—in which case, premiums based on the loss records for firms should provide a reasonably satisfactory guide to investment in hazard protection. Unfortunately, such a system would place overwhelming underwriting and actuarial burdens on private insurance providers. It is likely that few, if any, would choose to provide such coverage. Consequently, some economists have proposed a pure accident tax and public compensation scheme as an alternative to private insurance. Others argue for the efficiency of a system of strict consumer liability for product-related damages, but this model appears to contain unrealistic assumptions about consumer knowledge and behavior. Indeed, one of the biggest concerns with any of the information-type strategies is the question of the intended users' ability and willingness to use information rationally.

Another broad class of circumstances that has compelled government intervention occurs where information about relevant product or job characteristics is inherently inadequate for some reason. This may be because the relevant causal relationships involved are poorly understood and not easily researchable. This may also occur because the information that can be produced is too technical and probabilistic in nature to be utilized properly by the layperson. In such cases, information provision alone may not be a viable strategy. Governments may sponsor research to improve the information base but, for periods of time, important information may be unavailable or inadequate. In such circumstances, governments have not been hesitant to set product, process, and performance specifications, to establish permissible standards for workplace contaminants, and to promulgate outright bans on particular products and materials. Although such regulatory interventions have been subjected to substantial criticism, the ideas supporting them often make good economic as well as political sense. Where information is complex and processing costly and individual risk preferences do not vary too widely in the relevant population, government is likely to be in the best position to carry out whatever analysis is possible and to establish efficient standards for society as a whole.

A third set of circumstances that has stimulated government regulatory control is characterized by information that is at least potentially both adequate and interpretable—thus there is no market failure—but where at least some individuals choose to ignore it. Here, regulation often attempts to protect people from themselves, that is, from the consequences of their own actions.

Examples would include mandatory seatbelt laws, mandatory motorcycle helmet laws, and prohibitions on the use of psychoactive drugs the effects of which are known. Of course, regulation of this type also seeks to protect society from some of the external effects that unregulated behavior would cause and also may serve an information function by making it clear that society regards the behavior in question to involve substantial risk. However, there is clearly an element of government paternalism behind most of this type of regulation.

Unfortunately, but not surprisingly, it is difficult to evaluate the benefits of either information-provision or standard-setting strategies, especially after the fact. Isolating the effect of improved information and demand for the products and services affected for the purpose of comparing the resultant increases in welfare at the prevailing market price to the costs of providing the information is likely to be very difficult in most cases.[5] Accurate evaluation of both costs and benefits is usually problematic where standard-setting regulation is involved. Most of the costs of this type of regulation are borne not by the public but by producers and consumers. Methodology has been developed for calculating some of these costs, but the costs associated with long-term shifts in production, consumption, and other behavior patterns are very hard to assess. The difficulties on the benefit side are usually even greater. If good information about the relationship between the amounts consumes of the regulated activity or product and costs or benefits could be developed, it would probably be unnecessary to regulate with the standard-setting approach. Information-provision or market incentive approaches would appear to be more efficient.

## EVALUATING THE RELATIVE EFFECTIVENESS OF REGULATION

A number of attempts have been made to assess empirically the benefits and costs of regulatory standards. Studies of the benefits and costs of air quality standards were noted earlier. Perhaps the most interesting analysis of the effects of various intervention strategies to protect the environment, health, and safety, including information provision and standard setting and enforcement, is

Lewis-Beck and Alford's (1980, pp. 745-756) longitudinal study of coal-mining fatalities. Their analysis looked at mine safety in four distinct periods:

1. 1932-1941   No intervention.
2. 1941-1952   Federal mine inspectors gain access to all mine operations, powers limited to providing advice to mine operators and workers; safety recommendations not mandatory.
3. 1952-1969   Inspectors given broad powers to mandate safety measures aimed at preventing major disasters (10% of all coal-mining fatalities); inspectors were excluded from mines employing fewer than 15 miners (80% of all mines) and evidently prohibited from offering unsolicited safety advice to either operators or workers.
4. 1969-1976   Enforcement powers of federal inspectors much expanded, and a detailed set of health and safety regulations made mandatory for all mines.

During the first period, coal-mine fatality rates were higher and stable. During the second they fell substantially. They stabilized again during the third period and fell dramatically in the fourth.

These results appear to demonstrate the potential effectiveness of both information-provision and regulatory strategies. The effectiveness of nonmandatory safety recommendations is very probably explained by the prior ignorance of both operators and workers. Both were likely unaware of a substantial number of specific hazards in the workplace and, even more important (particularly where small operators were concerned), did not know how to correct them. Furthermore, once workers were informed of hazards in the workplace they could (and very likely did) bring economic pressures to bear on their employers to correct these hazards when it was in their interests to do so.

It should also be noted that under information provision, productivity increases in below-ground mines were realized at roughly the same rate as in preceding and following periods.

Comparing periods three and four, the most salient outcome is the reduction in fatalities following a substantial increase in regulatory effort, scope, and coverage. However, unlike in the 1941-1952 period, this benefit was achieved at a very substantial cost.

According to one estimate, deep mining costs (in constant dollars) more than doubled as a result of the implementation of the 1969 mine safety legislation (see Newcomb, 1978; Gorden, 1978).

In other areas, a model of drug industry regulation was developed to derive hypotheses about the patterns of demand for drugs after the 1962 amendments to the Food and Drug Act (see Pelzman, 1973). This research argued that regulation under the 1962 amendments raised innovation costs, reduced the number of new drugs on the market, and caused a net welfare loss to society. Other studies also analyzed consumer product Safety Commission (CPSC) regulation (see Cornell, Noll, and Weingast, 1976). They argue that the database maintained by the commission is inadequate and, due to other factors, is impossible to measure the impact of most CPSC regulation. Cases are noted where product hazard regulation was clearly successful (crib safety regulation, for example), but the conclusion based on limited evidence available is that most CPSC regulatory standards have higher costs then benefits (Cornell et al., 1976).

The Occupational Safety and Health Administration (OSHA), in the past and presently, attracts considerable attention from researchers. Unfortunately, a new data system on industrial industries was established at the birth of the agency, so that before-after comparisons of OSHA impacts are limited. In particular, workers' compensation data on injuries appear to have serious flaws. There is a great deal of work yet to be done, much of it basic scientific research, on occupational health hazards. Good benefits estimates are generally hard to develop, and the problems of cost assessment associated with shifts in production, consumption, and other behavior patterns remain. Empirical studies to measure the overall impact of OSHA standards on industrial accidents have thus far been unable to discern any impact. Benefit-cost analyses of specified OSHA standards attempted by the U.S. Council on Wage and Price Stability in the 1970s generally estimated costs to exceed benefits, using plausible assumptions about the value of various attributes of benefits (see Smith, 1976).

These findings do not indicate necessarily that regulation in this area is a failure. Several past studies pointed to ways in which OSHA, or its watchdogs in Congress, could improve performance. One step would be to increase the expected costs to firms of noncompliance with OSHA standards. Fines are often set so low and inspections so infrequent that compliance for most firms is irrational in economic terms (see Mendelhoff, 1979). Other studies make persuasive cases for a shift in priorities for OSHA to long-term occupational health problems, where the tools at OSHA's disposal are likely to have a larger net impact.

As in other areas of regulatory policy, evidence suggests the effectiveness of decentralized strategies such as provision of job hazard information to workers and the use of injury taxes to induce employers to invest in safety (see Smith, 1974). Problems related to the efficiency of an injury tax have been identified, but sound reasons remain to explore further the applicability of decentralized regulatory approaches, especially in light of the unattractiveness of coercive bureaucratically administered standards and the steady accretion of knowledge regarding the impact of hazards. Indeed, Cornell, Noll, and Weigast (1976) long ago argued that substantially increased investments in research may have the highest payoff among options open to occupational safety and health regulatory agencies.

An increase in knowledge about relationships between worker health and safety and the effects of government to correct imperfections in markets for information would seem necessary in order to proceed further in this area. On one hand, it is appealing to believe that provision of information is a sound alternative to regulation. On the other, we must acknowledge that, in many cases, the provision of information can be more costly than regulation, yet may produce similar results. If a public agency is able to collect, evaluate, and disseminate information more efficiently than the market, there appears to be sufficient justification for public provision of information. It should also follow that if it is less costly to set a standard or to ban a product than to inform people, then regulation is preferable to information provision. Consequently, the question becomes: When is it more costly to inform people? The initial answer is that it will be more costly whenever more information is required. However, it is somewhat tautological to specify that more information is required to deal with complex decision problems. It may clarify the search for an answer if we clarify the definition of a complex decision problem. First, a decision problem involves a choice between alternative actions, each of which will produce different outcomes. The decision-maker wishes to obtain the most preferred outcome. Second, the greater the uncertainty about the elements of the decision problem (i.e., uncertainty about the status quo, the range of alternatives, the relationship between alternative actions and outcomes, and the utility of alternative outcomes), the greater the complexity of the decision problem. Therefore, to note that we lack information is to indicate that we are less certain.

Given this understanding, government may reduce the complexity of the decision problem facing individuals in private market transactions in one of two ways: by ensuring that individual consumers or decision makers understand the relationships between actions and outcomes, or by eliminating alternatives from consideration. If government chooses the former, the cost of that choice may be measured in terms of resources used to collect, evaluate, and disseminate information to the public. If government chooses to regulate, part of the cost of this choice may be measured in terms of the resources used to establish and enforce regulations. However, a significant portion of the cost will result from reduced satisfaction on the part of some individuals, that is, those who would choose the prohibited alternative and would not err in this choice. An example of this is the cost borne in mandatory automobile seatbelt regulation by consumers who would not wear belts without regulation and would not suffer adverse consequences from this choice, for example, where these consumers were not involved in injury-producing accidents. However, the benefits of regulation for these individuals must also include reduced taxes and other payments to support the provision of medical care to consumers injured as a result of not wearing seatbelts, as well as reduced insurance payments. As illustrated by this example, determining the distribution and overall balance of costs and benefits of safety by regulation can be a complex undertaking.

Health and safety regulation attempts to reduce the incidence of outcomes that most people would choose to avoid anyway. But this fact alone does not justify regulation. Regulation that prohibits choices that would not be made is trivial. Furthermore, because individual preferences differ, it is often more difficult to determine which choices ought to be prohibited than it is to provide correct information. Consequently, a key to determining whether to regulate is identification of the cost of insuring that individual decision makers understand the relationship between alternative actions and outcomes. These costs are likely to be highest where a high level of understanding is required to avoid mistakes. This claim has long served to justify professional licensure, despite the ambiguity of evidence on levels of understanding required in order for consumers to avoid mistakes, as in health care and physician selection.

There is one area in which it is documented that individuals err consistently: the assessment of risks and probabilities. The evidence suggests that people are simply not good natural statisticians (see Tversky and Kahneman, 1974). People tend to be insensitive to differences in the probabilities of outcomes and the implications of sample size and predictability. Assessments of probabilities frequently are biased by the availability of data. In addition, errors are made in what is termed anchoring and adjustment—that is, people generalize between cases erroneously and fail to make adjustments for differences in circumstance. Furthermore, individuals tend to deal with problems sequentially, causing the proper relationships between low and high probability events to be ignored. Consequently, to ensure that individuals do not make mistakes when faced with choices involving probabilistic outcomes, it is not enough just to inform them of probabilities. In order to improve choice, decision makers must understand the implications of statistical decision theory. Furthermore, their understanding must be sufficient so that their choice reflects the knowledge of probabilities somewhat automatically. There is no assurance consumers or workers will develop such understanding. Even professional statisticians may not use their training in day-to-day problem solving.

A conclusion that may be drawn from research on decision-making is that regulation is likely to be less costly than information provision where difficult probabilistic judgments are required to avoid mistakes. The general rule that regulation will be preferable to information provision where uncertainties are great and information costs are high also may be generalized to analyze problems of externalities and market organization.

In a formal sense, the structure of decision problems faced by the producer of externalities parallels the choice problem of the consumer noted above. Market incentives change the understanding of relationships between alternative actions and outcomes. Regulation is generally intended to remove certain production alternatives from consideration. Of course, regulatory standards and enforcement procedures may also be viewed in terms of their impact on an externality producer may be influenced by estimation of the probability that violations will be discovered and by the penalty associated with such performance.

From this perspective, we may speculate on the manner in which the production of negative externalities may be reduced. For example, the standards and enforcement approach would simulate the features of a charge for externalities. Other incentives may be set by basing frequency of inspection on violation records to increase the administrative and other costs to the firm of violation, or by setting the size of the penalty relative to the seriousness of the violation. Enforcement efforts may be directed to where the costs of compliance are lowest and/or where violations are most damaging (see Portnoy, 1979).

If it is assumed that either regulation or economic incentives (the analogue to information provision) could produce the same reductions in negative externalities, the choice between these approaches should be based on minimizing the sum of search or design costs, bargaining and decision costs, and policing and enforcement costs. As noted, in consideration of these factors, there are circumstances under which regulation appears to be the least costly alternative. In general, it appears to be more costly to develop appropriate uniform design standards than to identify appropriate charges, but design standards are less costly to police and enforce. Consequently, where the externality-generating process is fairly homogeneous across many firms, and high level of technical expertise is required to determine how best to reduce the output of the unwanted externality, a "best available technology" standard should be optimal. Paradoxically, where large numbers of small firms are involved it may also be cheaper to tell them what to do and how to do it than to rely on outcome-related incentives. This is because it may be relatively more costly for them to figure out how to respond to the incentive than to comply with a directive. However, even the first of these generalizations is subject to exceptions. Furthermore, given how bureaucratic politics and administrative and budgetary policies condition the choice of regulatory strategies, the best practical solution may still be to rely on market incentives.

## MOVING TOWARD ANSWERS AND SOLUTIONS

We have employed a fairly traditional approach to market failures and believe this strategy is justified by its usefulness as a means of identifying potential remedies. We are persuaded by Arrow and Lind (1970) and others that the comparative advantage of markets or any other institutional arrangement may be reduced to a question of transaction or information costs and to the ability and willingness of those affected by these costs to recognize and bear them. According to Arrow, any institutional arrangement has the potential to reduce welfare losses associated with another, but before any conclusion can be drawn with respect to the advantage of alternative institutional arrangements, it is necessary to balance information costs under the existing arrangement with those of the alternative systems under consideration. And, although it may be useful for some purposes to distinguish between types of information cost-search costs, bargaining and decision costs, and policing and enforcement-costs these classes all reduce to a single one in that they all represent losses due to the lack of information (see Dahlman, 1979).

Furthermore, imperfect information may justify any form of government intervention. For example, if some Pareto optimal exchanges do not occur because of ignorance, government intervention may be justified—if government knows more than private parties do. However, we may not merely assume that government knows better (see Dahlman, 1979). Furthermore, markets work well enough in most instances that the burden of proof ought to rest with those advocating intervention. Unfortunately, the burden of proof usually rests with those advocating a change, any change, away from the status quo.

Regulation may produce substantial benefits:

- When it reduces negative externalities, resulting in a cleaner and safer physical environment. There, the benefits of regulation are reflected in a healthier and aesthetically satisfied public.
- When it reduces the number of mistakes made by parties to private market transactions by standardizing product or service attributes or working conditions.

We conclude that regulation is not an appropriate means by which to achieve single plant or industry efficiencies. Either some form of franchise and bidding arrangement or public provision of goods and services usually dominates regulation. If it is assumed that potential service suppliers better understand the demand characteristics of their market and the production and cost behavior in their industry, and if they can be prevented from colluding, then a competitive bidding arrangement should ensure the best supply arrangements possible in any particular market. If it is assumed that the regulators are as informed or better informed than are managers in the regulated industry, then private ownership has no significant function or responsibility to discharge.

Under conditions of externality, we conclude that regulation is inferior to the manipulation of market incentives and penalties as a means of reducing externalities. Incentives may take the form of charges (effluent taxes) or marketable rights. It is assumed that where producers can determine better how to reduce externalities than regulators, market incentives will outperform regulation.

Under the conditions noted earlier, it is asserted that public provision of information (or in the case of information asymmetries, certification, reassignment of liability, or enforced disclosure such as truth in packaging and labeling) will producer more efficient outcomes than will a regulatory program that restricts the range of goods and services made available, enforces standards of quality, or establishes maximum levels of exposure to health and safety hazards. Once again, if it is assumed that participants in private market transactions err only because information is absent, then public provision of information is preferable to regulation. This follows from the observation that public provision of information can meet social and economic objectives without removing alternatives from the market that some consumers and workers would prefer.

On the other hand, the information cost criterion leads to the conclusion that regulation is likely to be less costly and more effective than information provision where difficult probabilistic judgments are required to avoid mistakes. Relationships between risk, costliness or error, and consumer preferences provide perspectives on the choice of alternative institutional arrangements in other circumstances as well. With respect to direct regulation, we have specified some of the circumstances under which this institutional arrangement may be appropriate. Unfortunately, because of shortcomings on the part of the regulatory authorities, these circumstances are rarely fully satisfied. Nevertheless, we would, at a minimum, insist that where there is a fair degree of jointness in supply and consumption (where individual preferences are similar), total costs are likely to be lowest when purchasing and negotiation of the terms of purchasing and negotiation of the terms of purchase are delegated to a public authority or agent. These inferences are also implicit in our treatment of externalities.

Therefore, with regard to the advantages of regulation versus information provision, we conclude that where the probability of a costly error, rather than outcome, is high and consumer preferences are fairly homogeneous, provision of information is likely to be more costly than regulation. Likewise, there the probability of error is higher and remedies are similar, market incentives may be more costly than regulation.

If regulation has a comparative advantage relative to other government actions in certain instances, why is there so much criticism of it? One reason is distrust of government decision making in general. In turn, this distrust frequently reflects a distaste for interest group politics and its consequences, an appreciation of the short-term horizon that characterizes political decision making and cynicism toward the claims made about the public interest in political debate. Allegations of destructive competition, the desirability of a zero-risk environment, the infinite value of a human life, and the distributional benefits of regulation are all too often no more than disguises worn by special or exclusive interests.

A second reason is that the arguments presented here may not be entirely compatible with the static textbook models that most analysts (ourselves included) prefer. We suggest that models to take account of a wider variety of institutions, changing technologies and products, consumer preferences, and the implications of uncertainty for individual and collective decision making would better inform public policymaking than do abstract debates about the relative merits of regulation and competition or regulation and information provision. Unfortunately, such models are difficult to construct. Furthermore, as we have seen, their use seldom produces definite qualitative conclusions.

Nevertheless, we would speculate that so far as the choice between regulation and other forms of government action is concerned, the economists' bias against regulation reflects a very real tendency of government to rely too much on regulation. Regulation is the instrument most familiar to lawmakers. It is also consistent with the legal approach to problem solving in other areas. As Paul Portnoy (1979, p. 522) observes, "We do not tax robbers in the hope that they will find it economical to stop robbing." Consequently, regulation is often the first solution to a problem that lawmakers choose. Also, the information available to influence government choice between alternatives is often biased in favor of regulation. Paradoxically, given the logic of our argument, in making the choice between alternative instruments of public policy, government decision makers may be using the information cost criterion. However, it appears that they use cost measures that are not only inaccurate, but biased in favor of regulation (i.e., they tend to see only those costs that are captured in the government accounts). If only these costs are considered, programs that shift most of the costs from government accounts to private individuals, firms, and other levels of government will appear to be less costly than those that do not. In many cases, regulation results in such a shift. Furthermore, it seems likely that because the costs associated with the failure to choose the right institutional arrangement are not reflected in government accounts, whereas the costs associated with institutional and program design and development are so reflected, government tends to underinvest in analysis.

This chapter has provided an analysis of some of the most prominent objectives of regulation and the manner in which regulatory policy is designed to meet these objectives. It concluded in an attempt to indicate where regulation is likely to be most and least efficient in meeting objectives relative to alternative institutional arrangements. It also concluded that, in many instances, government relies too heavily on regulation, offering a few reasons to explain why this is the practice.

# Chapter VI

# *The Scientific Basis for Environmental and Related Regulation: Directions to Guide Policy Choice*

## INTRODUCTION

The theme of this chapter is that, in some instances, policy analysis may use science effectively in attempting to influence environmental, health, and safety regulation. This thesis is supported by explanation of some of the problems faced in attempting to define appropriate approaches to regulatory policy. This chapter is intended to demonstrate how policy analysis utilizes knowledge from the decision sciences, social sciences, and other disciplines to attempt to advise environmental and other regulatory policy formulation and execution.

The unabashed purpose of much policy research is to change policy, that is, to change the world. In fact, the principal standard against which much policy research is judged is whether, if implemented, it will produce greater positive net benefits than status quo policy. Also, policy research is increasingly asked to address implementation in addition to substantive issues. To some observers, requirements for addressing client preferences and implementation negate all arguments that methodological rigor is sufficient to make policy research scientific. Thus, much applied policy research will be judged by some as "unscientific." However, where policy research addresses client concerns and implementation generally, within the context of social problem solving rather than in attempting to influence choice by a single agent (a government regulatory agency and its director, for example), objections such as those raised above may be countered. In this instance, policy research, if it meets the inevitably subjective and peer-judged requirements of rigor, may be regarded as both scientific and contributory to the development of scientific theory in the substantive area in question.

While contribution to substantive theory in the area of environmental, health and safety regulation or any other field may be insufficiently "scientific" to critics who argue for a theory of policy science per se, policy research influences public decisions similar to the way in which research in the physical and biological sciences influences applications in space and weapons research, medicine, agriculture and other areas. And, it may be further asserted that much pure research in the physical and biological sciences is conducted along lines similar to the practical trial/error and judgmental model used in policy research, that is, "real" science is essentially trial and error and isn't always as scientific in method as assumed.

The remainder of this chapter investigates the scientific basis for setting regulatory policy. It attempts to suggest a strategy that, if followed, would increase consumer and worker environmental, health, and safety benefits and also would refine the effectiveness and targeting of federal government regulatory policy. Thus, it is argued by example, using a substantive analysis of regulatory policy, that a science of policy is not only possible and desirable, but that it exists in fact in the contemporary world. It is present in the many instances where scientific policy research attempts to influence government policy setting. The term scientific in this context is given to mean the systematic gathering, evaluation, and application of information to test one or more hypotheses that purport to explain both the causes of and the solutions to important social and economic problems.

## GOVERNMENT ENVIRONMENTAL, HEALTH, AND SAFETY REGULATORY POLICY

Accompanying the high increase in expenditures for medical treatment and health care that has occurred since 1960 has come a substantial increase in government activity aimed at reducing health and safety hazards in the environment.[6] This has been accompanied by considerable effort by individuals to increase personal health—increased interest in weight control and diet, exercise to manage stress, reduction in cigarette consumption, a dramatic shift to low-tar and nicotine brand cigarettes, and so on. Much of the expansion of government activity has taken the form of regulation of business. New statutes were passed and a number of new regulatory agencies created. In addition, existing agencies, such as the Food and Drug Administration (FDA), were given new responsibilities for protecting people from health and safety hazards.

There should be no doubt that the hazards addressed by these agencies are real. For example, experts believe that between 60 and 90 percent of all cancers are caused by chemical carcinogens in the environment and, hence, that they are ultimately preventable. Auto accidents are the third most important cause of death in the United States. A substantial proportion of these deaths are preventable (Page, Harris, and Epstein, 1976). Finally, prior to the establishment of the U.S. Mine Safety and Enforcement Agency in 1969 there were 100 deaths attributable to mine-related accidents and illness for each 10,000 man-years worked, a rate nearly eight times higher than in the next most dangerous major industry, railroading.[7] The rate is now half what it was and falling rapidly.[8] There also should be little doubt that the control of health and safety hazards in the environment is a legitimate function of government in a market economy. Their presence tends to reflect market failures of a type that can only be corrected by public intervention. And there is no doubt that, in the absence of public action, too little attention would be paid to the reduction of environmental and worker and consumer health and safety hazards.[9]

However, to say that some form of public action is justified leaves a number of questions unanswered: What is meant by "too little attention to the reduction of health and safety hazards"? Is it possible to "pay too much attention" to hazard reduction? On what basis should society choose between hazard reduction (ex ante) and post hoc remedies? What forms of public action would best accomplish a reduction in health and safety hazards?

Health and safety policy as presently implemented is frequently inconsistent and, perhaps that public intervention has gone too far in seeking to reduce some hazards and not far enough in seeking to reduce others. Further, public policy frequently fails to choose wisely between prevention and post hoc remedies. Also, the instruments chosen to effect a reduction in hazards are frequently inappropriate. These are significant problems. Their persistence reflects the complexity and obscurity of the issues involved and the difficulty of choice among complicated, often untried solutions.

It is increasingly understood that government cannot legislate all hazards of our existence and that, if it could, it would be too costly to do so. What government should do is less clear. To show that this is the case, this paper attempts to explain what might be called the regulatory ideal, why it is so hard to put it into practice, and what would have to be done to make it easier.

## Regulating to Minimize Damages

In theory, a "risk neutral, rational society"[10] will seek to minimize the sum of the damage resulting from environmental hazards to health and safety and the cost of reducing hazards. This means that steps should be taken to ensure that preventive measures are taken whenever prevention is less costly than the damages that would occur without it. This is the efficiency goal of public intervention to reduce health and safety hazards. Furthermore, a fair and "just" society would probably try to prevent sudden, drastic losses that fall on relatively few people. This is one facet of the equity goal of public intervention in this area (Cornell et al., 1976). In theory, there is no conflict between these two goals. An efficient, just society would take steps to ensure that those persons who suffered injury as a result of hazards too costly to prevent would be fairly compensated for their pains. Indeed, such a compensation scheme would automatically provide the information needed to determine how much effort to spend on reducing various hazards—they would be reduced up to the point where marginal prevention costs equaled marginal compensation costs (Fisher and Peterson, 1976).

Finally, a just society would try to ensure that the costs of preventing hazard damages and compensating victims are "fairly" apportioned. This is the other facet of the equity goal of public intervention in this area. Once again, in theory, there is no conflict between this goal and the goal of efficiency; those responsible for making the decision causing the hazard should bear its cost. If the net result of such charges were deemed "unfair," this problem could be dealt with through direct income transfers.

Unfortunately, the theoretical optimum is, or is likely to be, unattainable in practice. Certainly the information needed to employ these theoretical insights is lacking. In particular, the relationships between hazards and preventive activities are frequently poorly understood. Indeed, many hazards have not been identified. Furthermore, in many cases it is impossible to say with any degree of certainty what is "fair compensation" for an injury. For many, the loss of life or limb may be incommensurable with money—the form that "compensation" almost always takes. And with regard to the consequences of many environmental hazards, it is practically impossible to assign responsibility for their cause to a given individual or firms. Moreover, even if this information were obtainable, it is likely that the cost of obtaining it, prior to formulating policy, would often greatly exceed the marginal costs of an imperfect policy solution. Finally, it might be noted that, although it can be argued that collective (particularly societal) decision making ought to be risk neutral, (see Arrow and Lind, 1970; Fisher, 1977), it seldom is neutral.

Does this mean, therefore, that an understanding of the theoretical optimum is irrelevant? Not at all. At worst, it can help us determine what we don't know that is important to the design of effective policies and, thereby, permit us to design policies that may compensate for our ignorance. And it can help us identify areas where further analysis can have a substantial payoff in terms of improved policymaking.

What must be known in order to minimize the sum of damages resulting from environmental hazards to health and safety and the cost of reducing hazards? First, one must identify the total damage schedule, identify the hazard reduction schedule with the least slope. Identification of the total damage schedule may be broken down into three separate steps: determination of the change in hazard level brought about by a change in government policy (e.g., the reduction in sulfate emissions resulting from the requirement that all coalfired generators have smokestack scrubbers); determination of the change in the incidence of adverse incidents (e.g., deaths or workdays lost due to illness) resulting from a change in the level of hazard—this is called the dose-response relationship where health hazards are concerned; and determination of the change in damage costs resulting from a change in the incidence of adverse events.

It will be noted that the first two relationships are clearly questions of fact, while the third is a question of values. This qualitative difference is frequently cited as evidence of the irrelevance of the formulation of the health and safety optimum (Kelman, 1981). However, this is not the case with respect to the first two relationships, perfect certainty (at least to far as means and properties of distributions are concerned) is theoretically obtainable—at a cost—through either the evaluation of ex post experience or ex ante analysis. On the other hand, we cannot, in theory, hope to be so certain about questions of value.

In practice, however, we frequently have a better understanding of this relationship than of either of the other two. For example, we can be fairly certain that dying is "bad," but we are perfectly ignorant of any number of hazards in our environment (some hazards have not been brought to our attention). Moreover, owing to the indirect consequences of public action, we cannot always know how much a hazard can be influenced by public action once it has been identified. Indeed, it seems likely that analytical efforts designed to reduce our ignorance about the value of life and limb might have a greater payoff in terms of improved decision making than would similar investments in understanding either of the other two relationships. This information would be relevant to policymaking about every kind of health and safety hazard, while information about the first two relationships, particularly the second, is hazard-specific.

What do we know about these relationships? What can we know? What are the limits of our understanding? What implications have the answers to these questions for policymaking?

### Determining the Impact of Change in Government Policy

The first decision to be made has to do with the selection of the appropriate policy instrument or institutional arrangement Furthermore, an array of policy instruments is employed to reduce hazard levels, although this purpose is not always consciously recognized. These include not only direct regulation but also mandatory compensation schemes, the assignment of property rights, and information provision as well. We have argued elsewhere that there exists an appropriate criterion for choice among these institutional arrangements and that we possess a fair amount of knowledge on which to base such a choice. With effort, we may know a great deal more. Unfortunately, our knowledge or evidence base is not at this time sufficient to overcome the legal and cognitive biases, that predispose political leaders and bureaucrats to choose regulation. Consequently, the importance of designing and evaluating alternatives to regulation must be stressed.

Nevertheless, we shall assume there that this decision has been made and that regulation is the right choice. Hence, the decisions that we are concerned with have to do with the choice of regulatory mechanisms and their configurations. Paradoxically, despite the extensive use of regulation as a means of hazard reduction, we know very little about the relative advantages of alternative regulatory configurations.

What do we know? We know that hazards can be reduced by directly prohibiting them or by requiring some corrective action to reduce them. We also know that the effectiveness of these prohibitions will be influenced by the effort made to enforce them and that, in theory and with considerable effort, regulatory arrangements may be so configured as to produce the identical hazard reduction outcomes that would be obtained under alternative institutional arrangements.

How much a given hazard will be reduced will not, however, depend simply on the target hazard level specified in the regulation. Where corrective action is mandated, the connection between the action mandated and the hazard level and the enforcement strategy adopted by the regulatory agency will both have a bearing on the amount of hazard reduction actually obtained.

Enforcement has two aspects: detection of violators and their punishment. Once responsibility for compliance with regulation has been assigned and the kind of standard selected (either design or performance), detection may be either proactive, based on inspection or monitoring to determine compliance, or reactive, with detection following the occurrence of damages. If detection is proactive, inspections may be comprehensive and continuous or random and sporadic. Penalties may either be tied to the cost of compliance or be punitive.[11] The probability that a sanction will actually be imposed is also a function of the algorithm used by the regulatory agency's legal staff in deciding which cases to prosecute, evidentiary rules, and, of course, the legal resources of the noncomplying firm.

It should be noted that there is evidence that firms will frequently comply with regulations whether or not they are enforced. Random inspection can obtain compliance levels of 80 to 90 percent. Comprehensive inspection, combined with an appropriate system of penalties, can increase compliance levels to nearly 100 percent. An example of this is the Connecticut Department of Environmental Protection's (DEP) enforcement program. In this instance, the DEP determined the cost of bringing each firm in the state up to "standard." A monthly levy was then imposed on each firm until it complied with the law. This assessment was based on the rate that would amortize the cost of bringing the firm into compliance with DEP standards and had the effect of removing the incentive to delay or to avoid compliance by guaranteeing, in effect, return on investment in pollution control devices equal to the return on an equivalent commercial investment. This does not mean that all that might be known about the trade-offs between detection and penalty is known. The DEP enforcement program may be seen as a limiting case— minimal penalties combined with comprehensive inspection. Other solutions are more common. It seems unlikely, however, that this situation reflects a rational assessment of alternative enforcement strategies.[12]

The fact of the matter is that each element of the enforcement strategy adopted by a regulatory agency will interact with all the others to determine the degree to which hazards are reduced. Moreover, the effectiveness of a given regulatory approach may be influenced by other regulations and other existing means of promoting hazard reduction. In some cases, elements of the regulatory mix will work at cross-purposes to each other. On the other hand, apparently flawed elements of the regulatory mix may interact in such a way as to compensate for each other's weaknesses. For example, generally speaking, the severity of the penalty should be made inversely proportional to the probability of detection. However, under certain circumstances, one might imagine that a combination of high design standards, reactive monitoring, and punitive sanctions might be nearly optimal, at least insofar as the behavior of the firms subject to regulation reflected an economic rather than a moral calculus.

In this instance, where the cost of compliance represented the least costly means of reducing a given hazard or where the efficacy of alternative means was highly uncertain, we would expect the firm to comply with the standards. If, however, the hazard could be reduced with certainty by some less costly means known to the firm, it would be free to choose that option. Only where the cost of abating the hazard substantially exceeds the expected cost to failing to do so would the firm take no action.

Indeed, one may not conclude that, simply because a regulatory agency sets some standards at too high a level or rejects less costly but equally effective abatement technologies, overall resources are misallocated. As we will explain, identification of the appropriate hazard abatement level and technology can be very costly. It might, therefore, make sense for a regulatory agency to behave in an outrageous manner when forced to specify standards, in a limited number of instances, to induce trade associations to generate reasonable consensus standards. It might even make sense for an agency to target its enforcement activities, not where problems are most serious, but where they will get the most publicity. The point is that, although regulation may seem a straightforward, even simple, approach to the reduction of hazards, to anyone concerned with trying to understand its effects, there are few, if any firm conclusions one can draw with regard to the potential effectiveness or efficiency of regulation in general. Instead, one must first specify a hazard, its properties (or more correctly, our understanding of its properties), a target level of hazard reduction, an enforcement strategy, and a situation.

Regulatory practice is another matter. The elements of a regulatory strategy are seldom combined in an appropriate consistent, organized fashion. More than anything else, the failure of the regulators to employ consistent, appropriate strategies is reflected in their failure to pay heed to a single basic principle of management: The best way to get something done is to figure out who is best located to deal with a situation and give that person the authority and the responsibility to deal with it properly.

This is, of course, both a diagnosis and a prescription. For example, we tend to prefer performance to engineering standards, in large part because we assume that firm personnel are generally better situated and motivated to figure out how best to meet regulatory targets than are engineers located in Washington laboratories. This same logic underlies our tacit endorsement of many of the recent innovations in the environmental regulatory area—bubbles, offsets, and so on—as well as our earlier favorable discussion of smog and accident taxes, marketable emissions rights, and the like.

Several factors explain the regulators' failure to combine target, standards, and enforcement into a coherent, efficient regulatory strategy: flawed enabling legislation, interest group pressures, ignorance. However, these factors may be subsumed into a single factor: The absence of external pressure to improve performance and very likely real negative incentives in undertakings that may improve the efficiency with which regulatory objectives are obtained, but that also involve some risk. For example, a MESA administrator who adopts a standard enforcement strategy may not be criticized for failing to maximize overall efficiency. On the other hand, if the administrator does undertake nonstandard procedures to increase overall efficiency and something goes wrong, he or she may be out of a job. The inability to appropriate gains from increased efficiency, combined with the high risks associated with error, simply does not provide bureaucratic officials with incentives to try to improve regulatory performance.

The interesting question here is: Why is this the case with respect to regulation? We would contend that the explanation usually given for the lack of incentives to efficiency in the public sector is not very satisfactory, that is, an inability to measure the consequences of an organization's activities. The fact is, as far as health and safety regulation is concerned, performance can be measured—environmental quality, imperfectly; emissions, more satisfactorily; workplace exposures to chemical hazards, accidents, and so on can all be measured. Furthermore, regulatory performance often is measured, and when it is, these measures frequently appear to influence regulators' decisions, especially with respect to the design and execution of regulatory programs. But if we cannot explain absence of incentives to overall efficiency or the misincentives that had led to risk avoidance by an inability to measure regulatory performance, how, then, does one account for the behavior of the regulators?

Students of public management tend to overlook the fact that efficient choice requires both cost and performance measures. This is the case because the absence of cost measures is seldom at issue. Nevertheless, proper incentives are just as likely to be absent where performance can be measured, but costs cannot be or are ignored; as where costs are measured, but performance cannot be or is ignored. So long as regulatory decision makers are more attentive to their own costs, the probability that any given hazard reduction strategy will represent the most efficient solution to the problem of reducing hazards is lower. This generalization may safely be applied to the decision to employ regulation, as opposed to alternative policy instruments, and to the selection of an enforcement strategy.

Even if the incentives were right, however, ignorance would remain a significant barrier to the identification of optimal regulatory strategies. Much more can be learned. Because the lessons that can be learned with respect to the use of these mechanisms can be profitably applied to a wide range of hazards, such research should be given a fairly high priority. At the same time it should be understood that, in some cases, reducing one hazard (e.g., local concentrations of $SO_2$ and particulants) will create new hazards (e.g., long-distance transport of sulphates) or lead to unintended behavioral changes exacerbating others. In the evaluation of hazard reduction programs, these indirect consequences ought not to be ignored.

## Determination of Adverse Effects from a Change in Hazard Levels

With respect to the relationships between hazard levels and adverse incidents, we frequently know far too little and learning more will be costly. As noted above, information about such relationships may be gleaned either ex post, by working backward from the etiology of accidents, sickness, and premature death, or ex ante, by testing products, chemicals, and so on to determine their hazard potential.

Where ex post analysis is concerned, considerable damage must be done before a hazard can be identified. And even after a great deal of damage has been done, it may not be possible to trace damages back to a single hazard. This is particularly likely to be the case insofar as health hazards are concerned. The causes of illness are seldom simple or immediate. Consequently, ex post analysis can frequently do no more than suggest possible health hazards, and then only after considerable damage has been done.

On the other hand, ex ante analysis is expensive, testing on humans may be dangerous, and testing on animals is often inconclusive (see Alexander, 1977, 1978). Even if testing weren't expensive, dangerous, or inconclusive, the mind boggles at the task of testing all products, chemicals, and so forth for their hazard potential. There are over 10,000 consumer products on the market and 50,000 to 70,000 chemicals in routine use. At this time, fewer than 1 percent of the chemicals in routine use have been partially tested. Moreover, there is increasing evidence that chemicals interact synergistically to cause some illnesses, including cancer. Obviously, there is no way to test the hazard potential of all the possible combinations and permutations of chemicals in the environment ($50,000 \times 49,999 \times 49,998 \ldots$). Indeed it is not possible to test the 17 or so new drugs introduced each year in the United States for synergistic effects (the number of theoretically possible effects is about 300 trillion) (see Schwartzman, 1975).

It is possible that the best strategy would start with ex post epidemiologic analysis to identify possible hazards and would then proceed to more rigorous testing of these candidates.

Where safety as opposed to health hazards are concerned, present techniques of ex post analysis and ex ante testing in combination may prove reasonable guides to policy. Workplace and product safety hazards can be satisfactorily identified through the analysis of clinical records and case histories (see Kelman, 1974). Laboratory testing can frequently isolate product or workplace attributes responsible for the injury and determine whether or not they can be corrected. However, actual practice is distinctly inferior to what is currently possible (Ashford, 1976; Collings, 1972; Kelman, 1974). In contrast, where health hazards are concerned, the prognosis must be pessimistic. What is needed here are intellectual breakthroughs in data collection, analytical design, and testing procedures.

Finally, even where hazard potential can be identified, it may not be possible to specify the exact relationship between hazard level and the incidence of adverse effects. For example, it is known that there is a statistically significant relationship between air pollution and human health (Lave and Seskin, 1977). However, the size of the effect and the relative importance of various pollutants are not known precisely (Ferris et al., 1973). This means that even if the value question were settled, a precise damage function could not be established. However, good estimates of the upper bound on the size of this effect are available, and these, combined with qualitative information on the shape of damage schedules, may be a sufficient basis for action. This is so because where the slope of the damage schedule is understood to be roughly linear, basing hazard reduction efforts on a good guess will not produce substantially inefficient outcomes. On the other hand, where the damage schedule is dramatically curved to the origin, small variations in the level of hazard reduction effort may be critical. Consequently, qualitative understanding of damage schedules is one of the keys to sound policymaking in this area.

Of course, there are some relationships between hazard levels and adverse effects that are fairly well understood. To cite some examples, the effects of radiation on health are fairly clear, (National Research Council, 1980; Sinclair, 1981), and reasonably predictable (Secretary of Transportation, 1976). In each of these instances, adverse outcomes are probabilistic. However, where hazard levels are specified, both the means and the variance of expected damages can be estimated with a high degree of accuracy. Nevertheless, it does not follow that where this knowledge exists, health and safety policy is necessarily more consistent or more closely conforms t o the regulatory optimum than in other areas. That this is the case appears, in part, to be due to an unwillingness to place a value on adverse health effects.

## Determination of Damage Costs Resulting from a Change in Adverse Effects

Analysts generally reject the notion that the value of human life and well-being are infinite, but there is no consensus as to the proper values to use in the assessment of damages done to human health. Indeed, it is impossible to hope that we might resolve all the puzzling issues that are involved in valuing injury and death prevention. However, it is not necessary to do so to improve public policymaking.

For example, according to Wilson (1975), some of the safety standards on nuclear reactors imply a marginal cost of $750 million for each death prevented, whereas the corresponding figure for highway maintenance activities appeared to be on the order of $20,000. Spending resources on the former at the expense of the latter seems ridiculous. Most would agree a life is worth more than $20,000 and less than $750 million. The question is how much more or how much less. If we could be reasonably certain that a life is worth more than $300,000 and less than $3 million and, if the estimates cited above are accurate, it is possible that the variance in the cost-effectiveness of public programs in the United States could be reduced to one-tenth of 1 percent of what it is now. In fact, analysis of these issues has progressed to the point where we can say that it is probable that the average value of a life falls between these two figures. Furthermore, it is likely that additional analysis can significantly increase our confidence in such estimates. Because this kind of analysis is inexpensive and is applicable to a wide range of public policies, not only to questions of health and safety regulation, it seems reasonable that this is a particularly attractive field for further research. The questions to be answered are: Roughly speaking, what is a life worth? Can injuries be compared with fatalities? and: When is one life worth more than another?

Without attempting to answer these questions it may be observed that it is doubtful that anything certain about social risk preferences can be learned from social decisions. In the majority of cases, it appears that social decision making is risk taking; for example, considerable sums of money will be spent to rescue a trapped miner, but much less is spent to reduce the probability that fairly large numbers of miners will be trapped (Self, 1975). At the same time we can cite a number of decisions that indicate significant risk aversion, such as nuclear reactor safety standards.[13] Indeed, if one were trying to impose some logic on the observed pattern of U.S. health and safety policy, one might conclude that it is almost as if a conscious decision had been made to assume that most favorable state of nature would obtain in a number of cases, the most likely in others, and the least favorable in still others.

It may be noted that such a pattern of responses cannot be judged wrong or irrational (on a priori grounds). Of course, if all health and safety policies were submitted to systematic, consistent ex ante evaluation, the public interest would likely best be served by risk-neutral decision making. However, where each problem is addressed independently on an ad hoc basis, where the basis for the decision reflects real uncertainty or fails to reflect a sound assessment of the probabilistic information that is available, the public interest may be best served by a mix of policies that reflects both pessimistic and optimistic, as well as neutral, expectations. According to Lindblom (1965), such an approach to policymaking may generate wrong-headed individual policies, but the sum of the consequences produced by the full range of policy decisions may not be too far from the optimum—particularly when the cost of obtaining, processing, and using information is considered.

It might also be noted that the appropriate response to new information is different under these alternative policy formulation strategies. Under the first, new information should be used to revise prior expectations. Under the second, it must be treated as the sole basis for the policy decision. Both strategies require a readiness to make changes as further information becomes available. The first assumes an efficient search for new information. The second takes a passive approach to information collection. It is assumed that wrong-headed policies will bring themselves to the attention of decision makers. Consequently, if this approach is flawed, the flaw is that it is biased in favor of attention to the immediate and the determinant and against the more distant and indeterminate.

Unfortunately, regulation's comparative advantage as an instrument of government action is greatest where it is directed at the distant and indeterminate. Perhaps, it is this flaw that accounts for the apparent inconsistency with regard to the treatment of risk that characterizes health and safety policy, in that it simply reflects mistaken risk assessments. Perhaps it reflects the sometimes strange concentration of interest group demands and alliances. Perhaps it represents real preferences. The point is that we do not know. Until we find out, the last possibility ought not to be ignored. This means that ex ante analysis of health and safety regulation should comprehend properties of the distribution of outcomes other than the mean. This can be accomplished through the skillful use of sensitivity and a fortiori analysis.

Most environmental, health, and safety regulatory agencies have the potential for protecting people from themselves by making it impossible for them to make the choices they might likely if they were fully informed. Again, this is a question of values—who should be protected from their own bad judgment and by how much? Regulatory paternalism is an issue that deserves more attention. This is not to imply that the sole purpose of a regulatory agency ought to be to determine the risks associated with a given job or product and to provide that information to workers and consumers and then let them decide whether they wish to bear the risk. In some cases, it is indisputable that a hazard should simply be prohibited (Kelman, 1974). The problem arises when a government intervenes *to require or prohibit behavior that people would choose for themselves if they were fully informed of the probabilities and the consequences.*

The automobile airbag issue illustrates some of the problems encountered when government tries to protect people from themselves. Opponents of passive restraint laws in the past argued that if people wanted airbags or other passive restraints they would demand them as optional accessories on vehicles. Because consumer demand in the past was underwhelming, opponents claimed that regulations requiring passive restraints were an unnecessary infringement on personal choice. They also claimed that the same degree of protection may be obtained through the use of manual seatbelts. On the other hand, proponents pointed out that passive restraints could save 8,000 or more lives a year. They granted that manual lap and shoulder belts, if used, provide the driver with about as much protection as provided by passive restraints and that they were much less costly to produce. However, manual lap and shoulder belts are more inconvenient to use.[14] An estimate based on survey research showed passive restraint standards to be about five times as popular with the public as mandatory seatbelt laws.[15]

If the facts are as stated, why haven't people chosen to buy air bag passive restraints in cars? To do so would be perfectly consistent with other choices regarding risks in the environment made quite frequently. One answer is that, as an option, passive restraints often have been expensive or unavailable at any price. With a price ranging from 3 to 10 times their cost as standard equipment, this implies a value per life saved of $360,000 to $4 million, which is relatively high. Even so, between 1970 and 1977, at least 10,000 airbag systems were purchased as optional equipment at prices up to $2,100 each.[16] Many more have been purchased at lower prices in the 1980s and early 1990s.

In the past, Congress forced the National Highway Traffic Safety Administration to delay its proposed passive restraint standards. Finally, the 1993 Congress reversed its policy and air bags will now become standard equipment, phased in through the 1990s. However, prior to this action, Congress implicitly placed a fairly low value on a human life. Similar decisions have been made with regard to automobile size standards. One can only infer that the voluntary assumption of hazard entered into these decisions. At the same time, it cannot be inferred that Congress necessarily has a great deal of respect for freedom of choice, per se. For example, the 55 mph speed limit implies either that Congress has assigned a rather high value to a life or that fast driving is not a wholly approved of activity, in some part due to national fuel consumption policy preferences. The latter interpretation is more plausible. The question must be asked: Do these decisions represent current social preferences? Further, how much weight should be given to social preferences, and when should they come into play?

An additional related issue has to do with whether environmental, health, and safety policy should be based on the average value of life, on individual willingness to pay (and, therefore, on differing tastes and perceptions of risk on the part of those it is trying to protect), or on some measure of the social value of the individuals and groups being protected. Our health and safety policies appear to reflect all these positions in different contexts. Finally, some policies appear to reflect the belief that some hazards are more awesome than others. In as much as the best evidence suggests that these assessments are in error, it is suggested that people care about the cause as well as the probability of death; they would rather drown, die in traffic accidents, or die in a coal mine accident than die of radiation poisoning. Here, too, it can be asked whether this is a valid perception or a post hoc rationalization of previous policy errors. There is reason for believing the latter. It appears that lifesaving programs that are wholly federally funded tend to place a far lower implicit value on a life than is the case with some regulatory programs.

Even if the largest inconsistencies in environmental, health, and safety policy reflect real preferences, it is not clear that these preferences ought to be incorporated in public policies. In the case of well-understood spillover hazards, they certainly should be. But in the case of worker and product hazards, perhaps they ought not to be. One of the more persuasive justifications for paternalistic policies in this area is that the high costs of learning about and understanding various hazards can be avoided by the delegation of this task to a central authority. If this is the purpose of such policies, shouldn't paternalism be consistent, shouldn't policies reflect the best judgment of the experts and not the uninformed opinion of nonexperts? Isn't there a conflict between the objective analysis of a hazard and its possible remedies and the interpretation of social values? If so, which is the proper task for the regulators to perform? To us the answers to these questions seem obvious and ought to guide public policy decision making.

## Prescriptions for Regulation

The promotion of environmental, health and safety is a complex and difficult task. Much of what we would like to know about environmental, health and safety hazards is not known. If we had more information about these issues, we could make better decisions. However, information is costly. This means that among the most critical of the decisions that must be made are those that have to do with how much and what kind of information should be obtained.

Eight factual propositions seem to us particularly relevant to the formulation of health and safety policy.

1. We can generally make a fairly sound choice as to the best public policy instrument to use to reduce a hazard. The market and the liability system can best cope with easily identifiable and avoidable product and worker hazards. Where hazard levels or consequences are easily measurable, tax compensation schemes of the assignment of rights are more efficient and less equitable than direct regulation. Regulation makes the most sense in uncertain areas with which market mechanisms cannot cope (such as uncertainties about the weather and complex, poorly understood health hazards).

2. Regulatory activities must be properly targeted. This means that regulatory agencies must have sufficient resources to carry out the research and economic analysis required to identify hazards and to determine the best means of dealing with them.

3. External review of proposed regulatory standards should try to determine whether regulations are directed at problems they have the best chance of solving (the choice of instrument) and try to determine whether the damage prevention effort proposed is roughly right given the factual information available.

4. Confidence in the "rightness" of the level of damage prevention effort is contingent on an understanding of damage schedules. Ignorance is most serious where the damage schedule is dramatically curved toward the origin. Where this slope is understood to be roughly linear, basing hazard reduction efforts on a good guess will not result insubstantially inefficient outcomes, regardless of the slope or intercept of the damage function. On the other hand, in the case of a program concerned with the reduction of harmful emissions, if the emission reduction effort is characterized by increasing costs and the do-response relationship is nonlinear, small variations in the level of the reduction effect will be very important. This suggests that if analytical dollars are to be allocated so as to obtain the biggest payoff, they should be, first, directed at obtaining a qualitative understanding of damage schedules. Quantitative understanding of damage schedules should be sought only where there is prior reason to believe that they are nonlinear.

5. Cost-benefit analysis can promote the objectives of external review. A key problem of administrative decision making is that the costs relevant to administrators are not necessarily the same as those that "objectively" exist after a choice has been made. The natural propensity to view costs narrowly has frequently resulted in the choice of regulation, where other instruments would be more appropriate. It has also resulted in both under- and over-prevention of hazards. The strength of cost-benefit analysis is that it forces consideration of a wider array of costs, thereby reducing the opportunity for public decision makers to let their personal cost and risk preferences influence decisions.

6. It is possible to assign reasonably consistent values to environmental, health and safety benefits. This is the case despite the fact that precise values of human life and limb cannot be obtained.

7. As a society we must be prepared to act on the basis of information that is available and to modify policy as new information becomes available.

8. To accompany the economic analysis of specific hazard reduction proposals, additional research should be done in this area. Our understanding of the problems encountered suggests the following research priorities:

a. Research to understand better the alternative forms of public intervention to reduce hazards. This includes the design of alternative mechanisms and systematic experimentation with and evaluations of tax compensation schemes, information provision, and others.

b. Research to find shortcuts for the identification of hazards and dose- response relationships. This means the development of quicker, cheaper tests, statistical procedures and sampling techniques, among other techniques.

c. Research to get better upper-bound estimates of damages and damage reduction costs.

d. Research to obtain a better understanding of damage costs.

If these actions are taken, and if this research is funded and conducted well, then a more systematic and scientific basis for solving environmental, health, and safety problems and for formulating regulatory policy will be available to government and private sector decision makers.

# Chapter VII

# Future Trends in Corporate Environmental and Government Regulation

The context within which corporate environmentalism is evaluated is critically important relative to the conclusions regarding the extensiveness and effectiveness of corporate action. An international perspective is appropriate for such research to investigate how corporate environmental policy inevitably is influenced by the regulations, court rulings, public opinion, and other variables that pertain within each national and regional, state, or local jurisdiction. The following section of this paper characterizes the context for corporate environmentalism in Canada and the province of British Columbia.

## BACKGROUND ON ENVIRONMENTAL POLICY IN CANADA

The context within which corporate environmentalism is evaluated is critically important relative to the conclusions regarding the extensiveness and effectiveness of corporate action. Consequently, an international perspective is appropriate to conduct such research because corporate environmental policy inevitably is influenced by the regulations, court rulings, public opinion and other variables identified above in each nation. In this book we have noted that some corporations have recognized that responsible policy toward the environment avoids legal liability and resultant costs for environmental mitigation measures. Corporations with responsible environmental policy may also achieve other benefits including reduced long-term costs for complying with government regulation and interest group pressure, and improved public image. Another prominent incentive to adopt a sound environmental policy approach for business is the opportunity to convert an environmentally responsible image into increased product or service demand and greater market share and profitability. These trends appear to be the same in the U. S. as in Canada. In fact, the context for the development of responsible corporate policy toward the environment clearly is North American and international and not confined to the borders of any one nation. The fact that many environmental problems are transborder in nature further reinforces this judgment.

Focusing on the Canadian context, government response to the new environmental consciousness of the public in Canada has resulted in the proposal of sweeping action at the national level and substantial reforms in provincial and local government. Environment Canada issued the Mulroney government's the Green Plan in 1990, which was given high priority but little financial commitment by the Mulroney government. The Mulroney government Green Plan is a comprehensive effort to assess environmental and economic relationships in virtually all economic activity in Canada in the future. Along with the Environmental Assessment Reform Package released by Environment Minister Robert de Cotret in June 1990, the Green Plan signaled Canadian federal government intent to become thoroughly involved in environmental impact assessment, regulation, and financing in a departure from present policy in Canada where, unlike in the United States, the preponderance of responsibility for environmental regulation resides with provincial governments.

Public opinion and federal government action in Canada is causing reassessment of environmental protection laws by several provinces, and more reform may be anticipated as the Green Plan and other initiatives of the Mulroney and successive Canadian governments place greater emphasis on federal-provincial partnerships. As proposed, the Green Plan would serve as a model not only for provinces but for North America and the world generally. The Green Plan emphasizes the international nature of many environmental problems and indicates the importance of relations with the United States on a number of environmental issues. Redrafting of the Plan in response to input from a wide variety of interests attempted to satisfy demands of environmental interest groups as well as some opponents to increased federal government legal initiatives.

The Green Plan, with its emphasis on "sustainable development" and other government action on the environment in the 1990s may have profound consequences for Canadian corporations as they attempt to respond to a changing order of environmental assessment and regulation, just as has been the case in the United States and elsewhere in the world. The Green Plan issued emphasizes that cooperation between government, industry, and other environmental non-government organizations (ENGOs) is necessary for implementation of the new order: "*Business* is an essential partner in the search for, and implementation of, effective solutions to environmental problems." In addition to placing much more emphasis on environmental impact assessment, the Plan indicates that improved methods are needed to estimate long-term economic valuation of the environment as well as of proposed development projects. Of particular note, the Plan would require new assessment of development projects in progress such as the James Bay II hydroelectric project in Quebec, and controversial river dam projects similar to those reviewed in the past decade in Alberta, Saskatchewan, and elsewhere in Canada and North America.

Given the context for evaluation of corporate environmentalism explored above, and the framework for analysis provided previously, the next section of this study reports on an initial attempt undertaken to fulfill the prescribed research agenda, a survey of corporate and government environmental practices and attitudes administered in Canada in August 1991. The subjects for this survey were 32 Canadian corporations with significant levels of operation in the provinces of British Columbia and Alberta, and selected other public/governmental organizations in British Columbia. Respondents were executives in these corporations with some degree of responsibility for development for implementation of environmental policy. Data on environmental policy in British Columbia, Canada, and the United States used in part to develop the survey instrument and to interpret the survey responses was provided by the British Columbia Business Round Table, the

British Columbia ministries of the environment and forestry, Environment Canada, and the U.S. Environmental Protection Agency.

## SURVEY OF CORPORATE ENVIRONMENTAL POLICY IN BRITISH COLUMBIA

To investigate the extent of progress in the adoption of environmental policy and planning in business and government in Canada, a survey was conducted of firms and public organizations operating in the province of British Columbia. The survey examined whether and how private sector and public organizations have instituted environmental programs in their operations, the types of programs and activities undertaken, and some of the effects of environmental program implementation where it has occurred including costs and utilization of environmental themes in marketing and advertising. The survey also explored some of the perceived characteristics of government regulation and asked for opinion on the federal government environmental Green Plan. The written survey instrument was administered in person and completed by members of each organization who self-selected due to their involvement in and knowledge about the environmental policy of their respective organizations. The position of those completing the survey ranged from high level executives with broad organizational responsibility to middle management personnel whose responsibilities varied from general management to production, direct service or sales, marketing, research, and included environmental affairs officers and administrators with similar responsibilities in some instances. Telephone follow-up of the written survey was conducted in several instances, but not for the entire sample. Materials describing organizational environmental programs also were collected from the entities surveyed.

The organizations in the survey initially were divided into two groups according to the sector of the economy in which they operated (private or public) and differentiated by size using by number of employees as a proxie. The sample consisted of 16 private sector organizations and the same number of public organizations. The business sample consisted of eleven large organizations (300 employees or more), three medium-size entities (50 to 300 employees) and two small corporations (less than 50 employees). Of the 16 private corporations, 5 operate as manufacturing, wholesale, and retail organizations, 3 are in natural resource extraction and sales, 3 are in the service sector, 2 are in transportation, 1 is in retail sales only, 1 is in construction, and 1 is classified as other business.

The public sector sample consisted of two types of organizations: 8 public corporations (crown corporations) and 8 government departments/agencies. Fourteen of the public sector organizations were large with one medium-size corporation and one small entity. All the 8 public corporations in the sample operate at the province level (Provincial Crown Corporations) while 4 of the government departments/agencies are federal and 4 provincial.

Survey results indicate that of the 16 private sector corporations in the survey, 8 have adopted a formal environmental policy, 5 were in the process of adopting such policy and only 3 had not adopted any environmental policy. In response to the question, "Does your organization have an informal environmental policy?" 8 replied affirmatively, 6 indicated negatively, and 5 said they did not know. Significantly, 11 of the 16 private firms in the sample indicated that they had hired or appointed an environmental affairs official, and 5 of those organizations with such an appointment had officials who had served in this capacity for more than 2 years. Three corporations indicated that their environmental officer had been appointed within the previous 2 years and an equal number had been selected within the past year. Clearly, these results substantiate the assumption that corporations are devoting more resources and people to the development of environmental policy and programs. In some cases this is a recent change while in others action on environmental policy has been undertaken in a formal sense for some period of time.

Inquiring into the nature of the environmental programs adopted by the sample private corporations, 6 of the 16 organizations had undertaken a formal environmental audit, with 4 of these audits performed within the previous year and two completed within the last 2 years. One corporation had an audit in progress at the time of the survey. Of the 6 corporations that had performed an environmental audit, 4 reported that part of the audit recommendations had been implemented, while one indicated that no implementation had taken place (one response unknown). Of the 9 corporations that had not instituted an environmental audit, 5 indicated that such an audit was planned. Thus, of the total sample of 16, 11 had either performed an environmental audit or planned to do so. The 5 corporations planning to conduct an environmental audit all indicated that they would institute both internal and external audits (performed by independent audit firms). Finally, half of the corporations surveyed indicated that they had conducted informal environmental audits internally, and only organization indicated that an informal audit had not been undertaken.

In response to questions about corporate recycling activities, 15 of the 16 private organizations had formal recycling programs in operation. All 15 recycle paper, 6 recycle metal, 2 recycle water, 3 have hazardous/toxic or other waste recycling, and 1 recycles heat. Additional materials recycled by corporations in the sample are oil (2), cardboard (1), and rubber tires (one experimentally). One corporation has invested heavily in energy conservation, achieving considerable savings, and all have some form of energy conservation effort. For the 15 of 16 private corporations with recycling programs, 3 make a profit from it, 6 reported that their firms broke even on recycling, 3 reported that the programs were costing more than they saved, and 3 did not have cost information available to respond. Regarding production cost impact from corporate environmentalism, 2 firms reported savings, 6 indicated no savings and the other 8 either did not know or the question was not applicable.

The businesses in the sample were asked whether corporate environmental policy was featured in their marketing and advertising. Six responded affirmatively, and 10 negatively. Five of the 6 responding positively indicated that the environmental influence was moderate while one indicated that it was extensive. Four of the 6 that apply environmentalism in marketing and advertising have done so for more than a year while 2 have implemented such policy for more than 2 years. When asked a more general question about the importance of environmental policy in their organizations, 8 of the businesses indicated that it was very important, 3 termed it significant, 3 described it as moderate, and 3 termed it either minor or not relevant at present.

In response to two questions of a different type, respondents in 4 firms indicated that they believed the federal government Green

Plan was viable while 3 thought it was not; 9 responded that they did not know. With regard to government environmental regulation, *none* in the sample responded that regulation was fair. However, 9 thought regulation was necessary and only 2 termed it too costly. Still, 6 respondents thought regulation was "too political" and 4 termed it "intrusive." Three respondents described governmental environmental regulation as "incompetent" and only 1 of the total sample of 16 thought it was "effective." Comparison between private and public sector responses to these and other survey questions is provided subsequently in this study after analysis of the responses of government departments/agencies and provincial crown corporations is presented.

Of the 16 public organizations in the survey, 10 reported that they have a formal environmental policy and 3 indicated that such a policy was in the process of formulation; only 3 reported no policy. Fourteen of the 16 reported that their organizations had an informal policy. Eight organizations had an environmental affairs official while an equal number indicated not. Six of the 8 have environmental officials with more than 2 years of service in this position. Five of the public organizations had conducted or were in the process of conducting an environmental audit; 8 have not instituted such audits. All 5 auditing organizations have begun or conducted their audits in the part year, and 1 reported that all of the recommendations have been implemented. The other 4 responded that the finding had not yet been implemented. Only 3 of the remaining 11 public organizations indicated that an environmental audit was planned. Six organizations indicated that an informal environmental audit had been performed.

All of the public organizations reported that they had recycling programs. All 16 recycle paper, 6 recycle metal, 3 recycle wastes, and 1 recycles water. Two reported recycling of cardboard. Other materials reported as recycled included plastic, glass, chemicals, oil, antifreeze, tin, aluminum, and computer printer ribbons. All organizations had instituted at one time or another some form of energy conservation. Three organizations reported recycling as profitable, 3 as breakeven, 2 ad costly, and 8 did not know. In response to whether environmental policy had reduced costs in production (given that only 8 of these organizations were public corporations producing a tangible market product), 4 responded that they had saved money and 4 indicated that they had not. Eight of the public organizations feature environmentalism in their marketing and advertising, 6 of these moderately and 2 extensively. Seven of the 8 have involved environmental policy in marketing and advertising for more than 1 year, 3 of these for more than 2 years. In terms of the relative overall importance of environmental policy in their organizations, 9 of the 16 termed it very important, 5 thought it significant, and only 2 termed it not important at present.

On the two questions relating to government regulatory policy and planning, 7 of the respondents in public organizations believed the federal Green Plan was viable and only 2 thought it was not viable. However, only 1 respondent characterized the Green Plan as "popular." Further, only 1 respondent of this sample of 16 public organizations, half of which are themselves government departments of agencies (4 federal and 4 provincial), described government regulation of business as fair! Eight respondents termed it too political, 4 thought it was burdensome, 4 described it as intrusive, 3 believed it to be incompetent and *none* thought it was effective; and only *half* of the sample characterized government regulation of business as necessary. Still, only 2 respondents believed government regulation was too costly. Further analysis of the survey will report differences between government agency versus crown corporation responses on the dimensions reported above.

While the sample size and structure of the survey are not sufficient to permit a claim of representativeness or validity for the applicability of results to businesses and government organizations in British Columbia, Alberta, or Canada, the findings are illustrative, interesting, and in come cases perhaps significant. Comparing the private sector responses to those of the public sector component of the survey and analysis of the total sample reveals some interesting findings. Thirteen of the two sets of 16 reported that they had or were developing a formal environmental policy in their organizations (26 or 82% of the total of 32). This finding in itself appears to be significant even given the limitations of this particular sample. Eight private firms and 9 publics report that they have an informal environmental policy; 8 (25%) of the 32 do not have such policy. However, the survey instrument did not define what constituted an informal policy. Eleven private firms versus 8 publics have environmental officials (59%), and 11 of the total of 19 in the entire sample of such officials have served in their positions for more than 2 years (5 private and 6 public).

Seven private firms had completed or have environmental audits in progress compared to 5 in the public sample (12 or 37.5% of the total sample of 32). Nine of the audits had been done in the past year—indicating that environmental auditing is a recent phenomenon. Fourteen of the total sample reported having completed informal audits (8 privates and 6 publics). All but one of the organizations in the total sample operate a recycling program (only one business did not). All 31 recycle paper, 12 recycle metal, 6 wastes, 3 water, 3 oil and 3 cardboard (no significant differences in frequency between privates vs. publics). This finding indicates that while progress has been made on paper recycling, and 37.5 percent recycle metal (including aluminum cans), not much progress has been made on other materials. It should be repeated that only 6 organizations recycle wastes. All organizations report some form of energy efficiency activity, but only one private sector firm claimed to have achieved significant savings.

In terms of the cost impact of recycling, 3 privates and 3 publics reported that it was profitable (18.8% of the total), while 6 of the privates and 3 of the publics operate on a break-even basis. It is perhaps significant that 9 of the privates versus only 6 of the publics profit or break even on recycling (15 or 47% of the total). Five of the total sample (16%) report that they lose money on recycling (no significant sector difference). Also, fully half of the public sample did not know whether recycling was profitable or costly versus only 3 in the private sample. The quick conclusion from these data is that publics are less cost-conscious than the private firms, which is intuitively understandable given the profit motive in business and absence of it in government. A somewhat more surprising result is that only 2 firms reported production cost savings from environmental programs while 4 publics claimed savings. Six firms indicated explicitly no savings while only 3 publics reported the same result. Perhaps the difference lies in the nature and extensiveness of the production processes in the private versus public firms. A breakdown by type of firm/public organization, product, and production activity would probably yield more insight and will be performed subsequently using the raw survey data. Still, the small sample size limits any claim of representativeness based on this analysis.

Six private firms and 8 publics apply environmentalism in marketing and advertising (44% of the total sample). Sixteen do not employ it in this manner (10 privates and 6 publics). These two results indicate a relatively higher application of environmentalism in the public versus the private sector, which is not in conformance with the general presumption that private firms are attempting to capitalize on "green" marketing as a result of the profit motive to a greater extent than public organizations without this incentive. Perhaps the influence of ethical standards and norms of good citizenship are slightly more powerful motivators in the public sector than in the private. However, this hypothesis is purely speculative and cannot be supported by the survey.

## CANADIAN CORPORATE SURVEY SUMMARY

Seventeen of the entities surveyed report that environmental policy is very important in their organizations (8 privates and 9 publics). Twenty-five (78%) of the total sample indicate environmental policy is very important or significant (11 privates and 14 publics). Only 5 respondents (15.7%) indicated that it was minor or not relevant at present (3 privates and 2 publics). This appears to be an important finding as an indication of the extent to which environmentalism has permeated organizational policy in both the private and public sector. This conclusion is supported by the findings on nearly universal recycling and energy efficiency efforts, the use of environmentalism in marketing and advertising, the extent of environmental auditing, the number of organizations with environmental affairs officials, and the fact that 18 entities report having a formal organizational environmental policy.

The results of the survey related to environmental regulation of business are somewhat surprising in that: (1) the view of both private and public representatives is so negative, and (2) that the public sector respondents seemed to be fully as critical of government regulation as their private sector counterparts. This is counterintuitive in the extreme. While 17 (9 private and 8 public) or 53 percent of the sample viewed regulation as necessary, only 1 respondent thought government regulation was fair and only 1 saw it as effective. Fourteen (44%) characterized regulation as too political, 10 perceived it as burdensome and 8 believed it to be intrusive. Six respondents (19%) indicated that they thought government regulation of business was incompetent. As noted, views on these dimensions did not vary much between private and public sector in the survey. Moreover, only 11 of the sample (34.4%) thought the federal Green Plan was viable. However, the division of opinion on this question fits better with preconceptions—only 4 in the private sector versus 7 in the public believed the Green Plan to be viable, that is, public representatives view the Plan in a more favorable light. Perhaps they are more confident in government planning generally than are their private sector counterparts, despite their notable absence of confidence in environmental regulatory policy and performance.

The results of a survey of 32 private and public sector organizations in Canada also were analyzed to determine the extent of environmental policy implementation in this sample. Survey findings support the conclusion that environmental issues and concerns have permeated the planning and decision processes of both corporations and government organizations to the extent that business and government leaders are changing the ways in which they attempt to accommodate the desire of the public for environmental protection and preservation. However, the results of the survey also indicate that it is too soon to conclude that the action taken in the private and public sectors in Canada will produce the outcomes desired by a significant portion of the public. Concrete action to protect the environment is needed to prove that private and public sector planning, policy development, and marketing is not hollow promise.

## FUTURE TRENDS IN CORPORATE ENVIRONMENTALISM AND GOVERNMENT REGULATION

What trends are discernible for the future with respect to corporate environmentalism and government environmental regulation? While the future is difficult to predict in terms of specific actions by individual corporations and governments, some trends are evident given the material researched in preparation of this book. The following sections attempt to outline some of these trends in the wake of the international conference on the environment convened in Rio de Janeiro in 1992.

## Corporate Trends

Corporations are currently implementing many of the actions noted next. However, implementation typically is uneven across individual industries and by jurisdiction, region, and nation. Some firms are quite progressive within an industry while others are not. Likewise, some industry associations are also highly progressive in attempting to assist individual firms and the industry as a whole to the new context for environmental action. The list below incorporates actions now in progress in a number of firms with activities that are only beginning to be implemented by the more progressive and proactive elements of business and industry.

1. Greater efforts to save on energy and waste disposal through research, investment, and development of better technology.
2. Greater attention to integration of all the environmental activities of the organization under the umbrella of an overall corporate environmental plan.
3. Increased effort at long-range environmental planning.
4. Increased attention to construction of facilities and production processes that are environmentally compatible and cleaner, i.e., increased investment in environmental protection.
5. Increased efforts to market products as "green" or "environmentally friendly."
6. More investment in market research to determine which attributes of products that are related to their "greenness" that trigger consumption and by which segments of the consumer market, i.e., more sophistication in "green" marketing.
7. Increased use of environmental affairs officers as shepherds for the corporate environmental plan to keep it up-to-date and to monitor implementation and regulatory compliance.
8. Greater effort to learn from the experience of other corporations on effective environmental actions and activities.
9. More attention to public relations, in addition to advertising, about positive corporate environmental

activities and benefits to local 'communities where corporations operate and sell. These efforts will include more integration of local community and interest group leadership into the process of gathering information on what the corporation should be doing to assist local interests.

10. Increased use of nonjudicial procedures for settling environmental disputes with interest groups directly involved in the resolution process as a means of reaching better solutions and cutting the litigation costs related to problem resolution.

11. Greater corporate efforts to influence the formulation of government regulatory policy prior to passage of regulatory legislation. Corporations already exert tremendous effort in this area but they can be expected to increase the sophistication of their efforts by proposing solutions rather than just trying to prevent any legislation affecting them from enactment.

12. Increased use of environmental consultants for planning, engineering, legal services and liability assessment, environmental impact studies, scientific assessments of the effects of exposure to various pollutants, dose-response relationships, and so forth; and for presentation of results to governments, boards of directors, stockholders, customers, and the general public. Corporations have increased their knowledge of exactly what types of services they need from consultants and the consulting industry has responded by diversifying to offer a wide array of services.

13. Increased sponsorship of research into alternative and more environmentally safe chemicals and materials for use in production, packaging, transportation, and distribution.

14. Greater time spent by corporate CEOs and executives on issues related to the environment. This effort includes greater attention to communicating corporate plans and actions to boards of directors.

15. Increased formation of committees of boards of directors to focus entirely on environmental issues, planning, and policy.

16. Increased efforts by corporations, stimulated by government regulators, to form markets for the use of recycled

materials and substances. With a glut of recyclables available, and a public increasingly knowledgable and willing to recycle, corporations will be regulated into using a larger proportion of recycled materials in their production and packaging. Increased investment by corporations will be required to accommodate such requirements.

## Government Regulatory Trends

The efforts of government regulatory agencies is driven by consumer pressure that results in new and more restrictive regulatory legislation, administrative law, and enforcement efforts. Similar pressure, however, often is not present in the government budgetary process to stimulate the appropriation of sufficient funding to implement legislative and executive mandates. As a consequence, many regulatory agencies are not staffed and funded sufficiently to perform as they are directed. This is particularly the case for comprehensive monitoring and documentation of corporate performance in the field, for testing of samples and reporting of results, and for enforcement in the field generally. Consequently, the public assumes that government regulators are more capable of detecting and dealing with industry problems than typically is the case. The public also assumes that legislation, once passed, is implemented fully when this is seldom true because of funding limitations and successful corporate or industrywide efforts to block or impede implementation.

Increased recognition of such failures is made by public and environmental interest groups that tend to take their complaints directly to regulatory agencies and then to court once they discover that the agency is either unable or unwilling to take action consistent with the full intent of the law as interpreted by the interest group and their legal staffs. In some instances, direct interaction between interest group representatives and industry appears to be more effective in resolving problems than the alternative of government and the courts. A trend appears to be emerging on a worldwide basis for more direct interaction between interest groups and corporations to at least determine the nature of the problem and to assess alternative mitigation measures. At best, such action and cooperation leads to a united effort on the part of interest groups and corporations in approaching government legislators and regulators to urge them to take actions that at least at the initial phases of implementation are compatible with the goals of both interest groups and business. However, this type of scenario is, at this point, much more the exception than the rule. Other trends in environmental protection regulation are outlined below. Some of these trends it should be noted are in direct conflict with others. This is characteristic of the complexity of the contemporary regulatory setting where approaches differ significantly by jurisdiction, region, and nation.

1.  Increased effort to put market-based regulatory incentives into practice to stimulate corporations to change rather than attempts to coerce regulatory conformance through traditional command and control-type government regulation. Increased use of marketable rights, pollution taxes and surcharges, and other market-based approaches will be undertaken in the future as governments learn that these methods are more effective than command and control in achieving long-term public environmental objectives.

2.  Increased use of command and control regulation in jurisdictions where public and interest group demand is sufficient to pressure governments into taking direct action to force corporate and industry compliance. The costs of such approaches are high, but in some jurisdictions it appears that a combination of public interest group political power and a disregard for corporate compliance costs fuels a vast increase in the degree of government investment in new and stricter regulations and enforcement efforts.

3.  Increased efforts by government to set performance standards to which corporations must comply but not specifying the exact technology that must be employed to achieve desired results. Use of "best available technology" rather than specifying the technology to be applied saves corporations money in the long term and tends to promote wiser corporate investment decisions.

4.  Increased use of command and control regulation that specified exact technology to be employed by industry

regardless of cost or cost-effectiveness in jurisdictions where public and interest group demand is sufficient to pressure governments into taking direct action to force corporate and industry compliance.

5. Increased initiative by government agencies such as the U.S. Federal Trade Commission to enforce and publicize standards for "green" (e.g., "recyclable") product content, marketing, packaging, and advertising that corporations must meet or withdraw products from sale.

6. Increased government regulation to force corporations to disclose in greater detail the material and chemical composition of products and packaging, the extent and schedule of biodegradability, the best methods of disposal, and so forth.

7. Increased effort to regulate corporate responsibility for products and packaging through the entire product sale and use "lifecycle." Such regulation attempts to make corporations responsible for product disposal after they have been sold to and used by the consumer. This approach includes mandatory recycling standards and processes that corporations must meet and extends corporate responsibility for collection, reuse, or disposal of used products and packaging so that public/consumer disposal of these materials as waste into landfills is illegal, with the corporation held legally and financially liable for collection and reuse or disposal.

8. Increased efforts by government regulators to cause corporations to assist in the formation or increase the demand in markets for the use of recycled materials and substances. As noted, a glut of many recyclables is now present, and corporations will be regulated into using a larger proportion of recycled materials in their production and packaging to stimulate price for recyclables. Increased investment by governments will be required to enforce such requirements.

9. Increased regulation of cities and other governments by state, provincial, and, in some cases, federal governments to reduce the overall use of landfills for waste disposal, and increased regulation of what can and cannot be disposed of in public landfills, with such regulation coordinated

with recycling standards applicable to corporations and the public.

10. Increased cooperation between public jurisdictions, including nations, to attempt to resolve international and transboundary environmental pollution and protection problems.

11. Increased competition between nations for corporate facilities siting and commerce, with the provision of pollution "waivers" by some nations and jurisdictions to attract corporate production facilities and accompanying economic benefits.

12. Increased incorporation of environmental regulations standards into comprehensive trade treaties and agreements such as the North American Free Trade Agreement. These efforts will attempt to enforce the concept of an "even environmental playing field" between nations. However, although these regulations and standards will be adopted, and dispute resolution methods specified, standards will not be enforced effectively in some jurisdictions, frustrating the intent of the agreements and creating a confusing climate within which international corporations will have to operate. This, in turn, will place greater responsibility on corporations and industry groups and professional associations to develop and enforce self-regulation under the threat of sanctions applied directly within industry. In some cases, industry will align itself with environmental interest groups to pressure governments to take action against specific firms that consistently violate government regulatory statutes, rules, and industry standards.

These trends are only a sampling of activities that are either under way in selected firms and government jurisdictions or are in the planning phase. Key questions addressed in this book are: Is there an emergence of a new set of corporate ethics? Are businesses cooperating more with governmental regulatory agencies now than in the past? Are we any better off for all of this corporate and government action? There are no easy means for answering these questions in a comprehensive manner. As is the case in evaluation of any socioeconomic trend, there are signs of hope for the new environmentalism in the corporate setting, and there are clear signals of failure and alarm. To say that there is an increasing environmental awareness among consumers and corporate executives is not to say that this concern has been effectively translated into action to make the air and water cleaner; to reduce the production of hazardous and toxic wastes; to increase conservation, recycling, and energy efficiency; or to have any impact on the staggering problem of waste disposal in a wasteful and packaging-crazed world. Nor can we observe with any certainty that progress made in the United States or elsewhere is sufficient to offset the increase in environmental problems in developing nations, the atmosphere, or anywhere else.

Part of the environmentalist concept is "one world," that is, that there is in essence an existential reality about environmental degradation. Whatever happens from Brazil or Eastern Europe, Russia, China, or Malaysia, or from pole to pole will eventually affect everyone on the planet. The issue is not *whether* effects will spread, but *how* and *when*. Deterioration of the Earth's ozone layer, the spread of radiation from nuclear power plant disasters, the sweeping destruction of the world's forest resources, the potential effects of the greenhouse effect and global warming—all these events serve to remind us that, whether we like it or not, we are all environmentalists in that we must try to survive and remain healthy on this planet.

Part of the question posed in this book is whether corporations are "part of the problem or part of the solution." The obvious answer is that they are both. Still, it is somewhat revolutionary to think of corporations, typically vilified by environmentalists as the creators of many if not most environmental problems, as part of the solution. Rather, traditionally, it has been the environmental activist or government regulator who has been characterized as the savior of the environment working to thwart the greedy scions of industrial wealth. However, in the 1990s the reality has dawned that, in fact, it is the wealth of corporations that must be combined with the money of taxpayers and private philanthropists to invest in environmental mitigation, clean-up, and protection measures. There is no avoiding the reality that corporations need to be a part of the grand strategy of environmental action in this decade and the century to come. Recognition that this is the case is a step forward from the environmental consciousness of previous decades, which gives cause for optimism even as evidence of impact of new environmental disasters and additional risks to health are discovered.

With respect to regulation and ethical behavior, the perspectives presented in this book suggest that ethics have played a role in causing corporations to develop environmental plans and programs. It would appear, based on the evidence analyzed thus far, that ethical standards of behavior are reinforced by the other factors of causal variables identified in this study. It may be speculated that ethical standards are reinforced by corporate concerns for cost savings in management of energy and waste, by consumer demand for environmentally safe and responsible products, by interest groups that have pressured governments and corporations through the news media and in direct lobbying to increase the allocation of resources to environmental protection and mitigation, by government environmental regulation, and by court judgments and rulings in support of the intent of regulation. Economic factors and government controls have worked to support ethical corporate behavior toward the environment. However, it is unlikely that ethical standards alone would have achieved the results produced by the combination of factors identified in this study. It is evident that some corporations and government organizations are making progress in developing and implementing environmentally responsible policies and plans.

This book also indicates how much remains to be done. We seem to be only at the beginning of the age of environmentalism as a significant motivating element of our world culture, despite the fact that the environmental "movement" in the western industrialized nations of the world is approximately 25 years old. Change in approach to environmental responsibility requires the interaction of economic, social, and cultural factors and probably cannot be implemented throughout the world by the direct action of government as much as it can be "orchestrated" by a number of parties, for example, committed individuals, biologists, engineers, anthropologists, sociologists, economists, philanthropic organizations, public interest groups, the news media, elected and appointed government officials and regulators, and public and private sector corporate decision makers. Such orchestration toward a common purpose—saving the earth and its inhabitants from destruction of the environment—will be needed in the twenty-first century to reverse the alarming trend of environmental degradation that has accompanied industrial and postindustrial development in the nineteenth and twentieth centuries.

# *Appendix*

## STATE GOVERNMENT TOXIC WASTE REGULATIONS: THE OREGON TOXIC REDUCTION PROGRAM MODEL

### Introduction to the Toxic Use Reduction Problem

Toxic use reduction is defined as:

> Changes in production processes, products or raw materials that reduce, avoid, or eliminate the use of toxic or hazardous substances and the generation of hazardous by-products per unit of production, so as to reduce overall risks to the health of workers, consumers or the environment without shifting risks between workers, consumers or parts of the environment (Ryan et al., January 1991, p. 4).

The need and opportunity for toxics use reduction programs has never been so great. Despite a substantial body of pollution control and toxic hazardous legislation, the threats to consumers, workers, and communities continue to increase because of a lack of enforcement and the accelerated production and use of new chemicals. According to Sugarman (1991, p. 3):

- Between 1940 and 1987, the production of synthetic organic chemicals in the United States increased from 1 million tons to 125 million tons—a 12,500% increase.
- Toxic chemicals are found in the body tissues of most, if not all, Americans—many of which are carcinogenic, mutagenic, or cause birth defects and other health problems (see Table A.1).

- Existing environmental laws suffer from being piecemeal, adversarial, and retroactive (regulating toxics in air, land, or water after they are produced—ex post facto). Toxics use prevention can be more cost-effective and reduce industry liabilities, as well as protect the environment.

*Table A.1.* Toxic Chemicals Most Produced in the United States

| Amounts and Associated Hazards | | |
| --- | --- | --- |
| Chemical | Amount Produced* (billion pounds) | Hazards** |
| Sulfuric Acid | 87 | A,Ch,E |
| Ethylene | 35 | Ch |
| Ammonia | 33 | A,Ch,E |
| Chlorine | 22 | A,Ch,E |
| Propylene | 20 | |
| Nitric Acid | 17 | A |
| Ammonium Nitrate | 14 | Ch |
| Benzene | 12 | C,K,R,Ch,E |
| Vinyl Chloride | 8.5 | C,H,D,R,A,Ch |
| Styrene | 8.1 | C,H,K,Ch,E |
| Ethylbenzene | 7.4 | A,Ch,D,R |
| Methanol | 7.1 | N |
| Formaldehyde | 6.4 | C,H,R,A,Ch,E |
| Xylene (mixed isomer) | 6.3 | Ch,D,R,E |
| Acetaldenyde | 6.3 | A,C,e |
| 1,3-Butadiene | 6.2 | C,Ch,D,E,N,R |
| Ethylene Oxide | 6.1 | C,H,D,R,A,Ch,N,E |
| Ethylene Glycol | 5.5 | Ch |
| Toluene | 5.4 | D,R,E |
| Hydrochloric Acid | 5.3 | A,Ch |

*Notes:* *U.S. production amounts obtained from recent articles in "Chemical & Engineering News" and from the Hazardous Substance Data Base, a computer database maintained by the National Library of Medicine.

**Chemical hazard abbreviations are:

- C  carcinogenicity
- H  heritable genetic and chromosomal mutations
- D  developmental toxicity
- R  reproductive toxicity
- Ch  chromic toxicity
- A  acute toxicity
- E  envirotoxicity
- N  neurotoxicity

If one of these chemical hazards is marked next to a chemical, then for that chemical, available data support a concern that the chemical is or may be associated with that health threat.

*Source:* (Sugarman, March 1991)

Therefore, existing pollution control laws can be augmented with a more proactive, cost-effective system designed to prevent toxics generation, disposal, and related worker, consumer, community, and environmental contamination.

In general, toxics use reduction can be achieved in five ways (Sugarman, March 1991, p. 4).

1. Substitute nontoxic for toxic chemicals in production processes;
2. Redesign products to reduce toxics in production processes and products;
3. Substitute new, efficient, nontoxic production machinery and processes for older, more toxic production processes;
4. Improved housekeeping—monitor for and plug the leaks;
5. Recycle toxic materials in production processes.

In the United States, in 1989, Oregon and Massachusetts were the two first states to pass toxic use reduction legislation. The experiences of Oregon in developing and implementing a toxic use program will be the central focus of this appendix. Although Oregon is by no means the largest producer of toxic materials in the United States (see Table A.2), the state has a reputation for progressive environmental management (including bottle bills, beach bills, bike bills, billboard bills [the "B" bills], land use and energy planning—to name a few.

Oregon continues to have many toxics problems, however. The Oregon Department of Environmental Quality has identified over 200 hazardous waste sites and over 100 cases of ground water contamination in Oregon. In 1990, the state fire marshall reported 347 hazardous waste-related accidents (approximately 38% in transportation) that created substantial public risk (OSPIRG, Fact Sheet).

According to OSPIRG (1991), an estimated 31 million pounds of toxic material was released into the air, land, and waters of Oregon. Figure A.1 documents the releases to air, water, land, and publicly owned treatment works (POTWs). Only 9 percent, or 3 million pounds, of the toxic chemicals were transported to treatment, storage, and disposal facilities.

Figures A.2 and A.3 summarize toxic releases by industry type and amount. Paper products (40%), advanced instrumentation (12%), and primary metals (11%) account for over 63% of the releases in the state.

*Table A.2.*  Toxics Use and Releases of Top 36 States

| State | Toxic Use (Estimate in pounds) | Release (Pounds) |
|---|---|---|
| Louisiana | | 7411 Billion |
| Texas | 10 to 100 Billion | 724 Billion |
| Ohio | | 375 Billion |
| | | |
| Illinois | | 251 Million |
| Florida | | 250 Million |
| Tennessee | | 250 Million |
| Michigan | | 232 Million |
| California | | 202 Million |
| Virginia | | 197 Million |
| New Jersey | | 193 Million |
| Kansas | 1 to 10 Billion | 174 Million |
| New York | | 172 Million |
| North Carolina | | 137 Million |
| Georgia | | 130 Million |
| Kentucky | | 130 Million |
| Mississippi | | 120 Million |
| Alabama | | 84 Million |
| Arkansas | | 72 Million |
| Massachussetts | | 71 Million |
| Minnesota | | 66 Million |
| West Virginia | | 58 Million |
| | | |
| Indiana | | 276 Million |
| Missouri | | 184 Million |
| Utah | | 137 Million |
| Wisconsin | | 100 Million |
| Arizona | | 75 Million |
| Iowa | | 60 Million |
| Connecticut | 100 Million to 1 Billion | 53 Million |
| Washington | | 50 Million |
| Oregon | | 34 Million |
| Maryland | | 33 Million |
| Maine | | 22 Million |
| Colorado | | 21 Million |
| Idaho | | 15 Million |
| Delaware | | 11 Million |
| Nevada | | 4.9 Million |

*Source:*  Sugarman (1991).

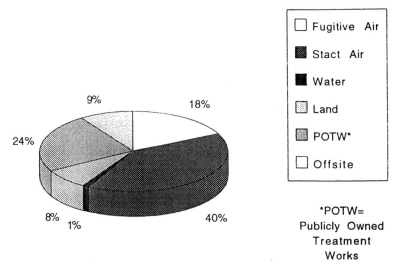

*Figure A.1.* Media Breakdown for Oregon Releases (Sugarman, March 1991)

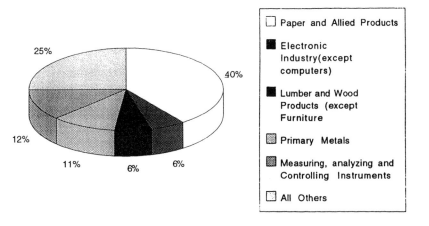

*Figure A.2.* Toxic Releases by Industry Type (Sugarman, March 1991)

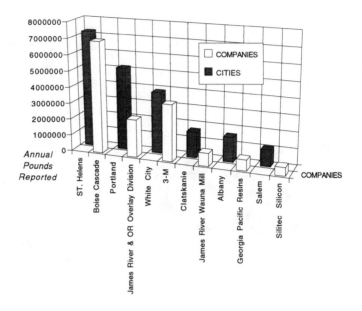

*Figure A.3.* Oregon Cities with Largest Toxic Releases and Largest Corporate Contributor (Modified from Sugarman, March 1991)

## Oregon's Toxic Use Reduction and Hazardous Waste Reduction Acts

Recognizing that there was a problem of toxics use in Oregon, the state legislature, in 1989, passed the Oregon Toxic Use Reduction and Hazardous Waste Reduction Act (HB 3515). The Act addressed toxic chemical usage from start (toxics use) to finish (hazardous waste generation). The bill, which unanimously passed the Oregon State Legislature, stated that the best way to minimize toxic exposures to workers in the workplace were to (DEQ, ND):

- Provide technical assistance to affected industries,
- Monitor the use of toxic substances and the generation of hazardous waste,
- Required comprehensive toxics use and waste planning of affected industries to develop measurable performance goals.

The law applies to three types of business (DEQ, ND):

1.  Large users of toxic chemicals required to report under the federal Community Right-to-Know program (SARA, Title III, Section 313,
2.  Fully regulated hazardous waste generators generating more than 2200 pounds per month of hazardous waste (or 2.2 pounds per month of "acutely" hazardous waste),
3.  Small quantity (between 220-2200 pounds per month) hazardous waste generators.
    "Conditionally-exempt generators" of hazardous waste are not required to develop plans, but are eligible for technical assistance (see Attachment 1 for further definition).

The "qualifying" hazardous waste generators in Oregon are required to develop toxics use and hazardous waste reduction plans. These plans consist of (DEQ, ND):

1.  A written policy statement from corporate management indicating support for the planning process and a commitment to implement plan goals,
2.  A written statement of plan goals, objectives, and scope,
3.  Quantitative reduction goals for certain toxic substances and wastes,
4.  An analysis of toxic use and waste streams and development of a cost-accounting system,
5.  Identification of reduction alternatives and strategies,
6.  Establishment of employee awareness and training programs,
7.  Implementation of technically and economically sound toxic use and hazardous waste reduction alternatives; and on-going institutionalization of the program,
8.  Submitting an annual report (including plan description and annual progress) to the Oregon Department of Environmental Quality (DEQ). 3.

### Program Administration and Enforcement

The Oregon DEQ was given authority to administer the new program. The DEQ has expanded its waste reduction technical assistance program to include on-site industry assistance, training workshops, an information clearinghouse, and a public recognition program for successful industries (see Attachment 2).

It is important to note that sensitive technical information submitted by industries are not a part of public records. DEQ staff findings are only made available to the public if the DEQ finds planning deficiencies and a reluctance to correct them. If this is the case, the DEQ can conduct a public hearing to formulate an adequate use and waste reduction plan (DEQ, ND). 4.

Case Studies: The "Governor's Awards"

A strong incentive was built into the Oregon program through the development of the "Oregon Governor's Award for Toxics Use Reduction." Appendix C summarizes the program and application and eligibility criteria. The two 1991 winners were:

- Consolidated Freightways of Portland—for establishing a toxic use and hazardous waste reduction "Excel Committee" and for developing a nontoxic chemical substitute in a wash unit.
- Wacker Siltronic Corporation—for elimination of TCE silicon wafer cleaning.

In 1992, the awards were given to:

- Intel—for overall management systems including elimination of Freon 113 in printed circuit board cleaning processes and for reducing phosphoric acid wastes.
- Hewlett-Packard—for eliminating CFCs in its processes, eliminating nickel waste disposal through reuse, and reduced use of TCA and TCE.
- Siltec Corporation—eliminated CFCs, TCA, and TCE in silicon wafer cleaning processes; reducing use of ammonium hydroxide, hydrogen peroxide; and reducing chronic acid wastes.
- Oregon Department of Transportation, Highway Division Support Services Branch, Salem—for establishing a "Management Advisory Committee," which has produced $30,000 a year in cost savings through use and waste reductions.
- Tigard Auto Body—reusing paints and reducing paint wastes; re-using and recycling antifreeze; and reducing air particulate emissions. (DEQ, 9/15/92 News Release)

Toxic Use and Waste Reduction Program Benefits

A Toxic Use and Waste Reduction Program and result in long-term economic benefit from using less, buying less, disposing less and reducing the liability of toxic effects. Implementing a corporate strategy to reduce wastes can provide other valuable benefits to the Corporation:

- Improve corporate image
- Boost staff loyalty and commitment internally
- Increase sales of products and services
- Reduce risk of liability of health and environmental damage
- Minimize impact to environment
- Satisfy investor and lender environmental liability concerns
- Decrease costs in purchasing toxic chemicals
- Decrease cost for waste management
- Reduce the number of accidents, both on-site and off-site
- Reduce routine and occupational exposures to toxic materials
- Reduce consumer exposures to toxic-containing products. (modified from Peat et al. 1991)

Program Evaluation

To date, 13 states have enacted some type of a pollution prevention law. In 1991, three national environmental groups conducted a comparative study of 11 of these laws (National Environmental Law Center (NELC) and Center for Policy Alternatives, January 1991). The study used a panel of experts to evaluate the effectiveness of each program (using six criteria) in toxics use reduction (see Table A.3). The expert panel rated Oregon's program second to Massachusetts' because of less involvement and enforcement authority and the fact that Oregon's program addresses waste *and* use reduction—not just use reduction (this "definition" criteria was ranked as the most important by the expert panel). Although the Oregon law gives clear preference to use reduction over waste reduction, several panelists expressed concern over how well a combined use and waste law would work.

## Table A.3. Rankings of State Programs Effectiveness

| State | MA | OR | IN | WA | IL | ME | CA | MN | GA | TN | MS |
|---|---|---|---|---|---|---|---|---|---|---|---|
| Definition | ***** | *** | **** | **** | **** | *** | ** | ** | ** | ** | * |
| Planning | **** | *** | * | ** | * | ** | ** | ** | ** | ** | ** |
| Reporting | *** | *** | * | ** | — | ** | ** | ** | * | * | ** |
| Involvement | *** | * | * | * | — | * | ** | * | * | * | * |
| Authority | ** | * | * | * | ** | * | — | — | — | * | — |
| Assistance | *** | ** | *** | ** | *** | * | ** | ** | * | * | * |
| Overall Rating | 6.9 | 3.6 | 3.4 | 3.4 | 3.0 | 2.8 | 2.2 | 2.1 | 1.9 | 1.9 | NR |

Key: **Ratings**

Average Score of:

| | | |
|---|---|---|
| Excellent | 8 to 10 | ***** |
| Very Good | 6 to 8 | **** |
| Good | 4 to 6 | *** |
| Fair | 2 to 4 | ** |
| Poor | 0 to 2 | * |

**Abbreviations**

MA  Massachusetts
OR  Oregon
IN  Indiana
WA  Washington
IL  Illinois
ME  Maine
CA  California
MN  Minnesota
GA  Georgia
TN  Tennessee
MA  Mississippi

Source:  Ryan et al. (1991).

150

Model Law

In 1991, the National Environmental Law Center (NELC) developed a model "Toxics Use Reduction Act." The following summarizes the Act, according to the criteria established in Table II.4. A complete copy of the Act can be obtained from the NELC in Washington, DC.

Criterion One: Definition

The model law for promoting toxics use reduction would be named the "Toxics Use Reduction Act." It would be a freestanding, multimedia law not tied to any particular existing law or environmental medium. Its sole foundation term would be "toxics use reduction," which would be defined something like:

> In-plant changes in production processes are raw materials that reduce, avoid, or eliminate the use of toxic or hazardous substances or the generation of hazardous byproducts per unit of product, so as to reduce risks to the health of workers, consumers, or the environment, without shifting risks among workers, consumers, or parts of the environment.

The definition should specify that such changes could be accomplished through input substitution, product reformulation, production process redesign or modification, production process modernization, improved production process operation and maintenance, or in-process recycling, reuse or extended use of toxics by using equipment integral to the production process.

It should specifically exclude: (1) incineration, (2) transfer from one medium of release to another, (3) off-site or out-of-process waste recycling, or (4) end-of-pipe treatment.

The emphasis of this definition on production process change, reduction of the use of substances, protecting workers and consumers as well as the environment (thus making it truly multimedia), and on not risk shifting are all important.

Criteria Two and Three: Planning and Reporting

The following section presents model law information on both planning and reporting. They have been listed together here so one can better see how the two sections relate and because there are many elements common to both planning and reporting.

*NELC Model Law*

The model toxics use reduction law would include the following requirements:

- Planning
- A focus solely on toxics use reduction, according to the model definition, with planning to reduce use and byproduct generation
- A statement by management articulating their support for the plan and waste/source/use/release reduction
- Analysis of technically and economically practicable options for reduction of use/emissions/waste/release generation
- A statement regarding the scope and objectives of the plan; often specific performance goals are requested as a method of fulfilling this requirement
- A rationale for why a company has chosen to address specific concerns
- Required of all facilities in the state that produce or use greater than 10,000 pounds of a Section 313 or CERCLA listed chemical for such chemicals, and of all facilities required to report to extremely hazardous substances under Section 312 of SARA for such substances
- Analysis of all production processes in which such a 313, CERCLA, or extremely hazardous chemical is manufactured or used
- Establishment of quantitative reduction goals for use and byproduct generation on a per unit of product basis for each production process for each chemical, plus quantitative facilitywide reduction goals for use and byproduct generation for each chemical
- Plans available to agency personnel for their review and analysis
- Plans to be signed off on as complete by state-certified toxics use reduction planners
- $25,000 maximum penalty per day for failure to produce adequate plan, criminal penalties for willful violations
- State may reject plans if not adequate
- Statements of why particular option was or was not implemented

- Updated biannually.

Criterion Four: Worker and Community Involvement

*NELC Model Law*
A model law would include:
- Focus on toxics use reduction.
- Provisions for workers to review plans and participate in planning, for hazard prevention committees to be required at user facilities, for workers to have access to toxics use reduction training, that workers may call for health and safety inspections, and that state grants are available for workers to hire toxics use reduction experts to assist them.
- Concerned neighbors and LEPCs would be able to review plans and participate in planning, to receive toxics use reduction training and assistance, to be able to call for and accompany environmental compliance inspections, and get state grants to hire toxics use reduction experts.
- Worker hazard committees would be able to temporarily stop imminently hazardous operations and petition state agencies to establish safe substitute standards where substitutes are economically feasible.
- Citizen suit improvisions, allowing citizens to sue companies that do not comply with the law, with attorney and expert witness fee provisions.

Criterion Five: State Assistance to Users

*NELC Model Law:*
A model law would include:
- A focus solely on promoting toxics use reduction.
- An effort to provide and distribute general information about toxics use reduction to users.
- A primary focus on providing assistance to groups of users using the same or similar production processes, so that the agency's expertise can be deep and applied to many users who will really benefit from that expertise, not spread out trying to assist many different types of operations. The agency would select and work with such user groups to develop useful technical and cost information on reduction

and then distribute that information to all users in those groups.

- A priority-setting system for deciding which groups of users should receive assistance first, based on their amounts of use, degree of hazard, and potential for reduction.
- On-site consultations to users by a group independent of the state regulators, so that trust relations can be built.
- Training programs which offer continuing education courses and graduate and undergraduate curricula.
- Financial assistance to help firms in need, which are good investments, to undertake reduction projects.
- Research and demonstration programs for priority production processes, either in-house at a university or through a grant program.

Criterion Six: Statewide Regulatory Authority and Reform

*NELC Model Law:*
A model law would include:
- A focus on toxics use reduction.
- State agency authority to set performance standards for companies' use of any particular process, in terms of maximum use or byproduct generated per unit of product, with standards targeted to what the best companies using that process have achieved.
- State agency authority to ban or phase out uses or particular uses of particular chemicals if justified by health or environmental data, with no mandated consideration required for economic impacts and with strong penalties for noncompliance.
- Goals for a statewide reduction in 5 years of 50% in byproduct generated and 30% in toxics use, applicable to 313, CERCLA, and extremely hazardous substances, and with annual monitoring of progress.
- Mandate that state enforcement efforts be multimedia in nature, including occupational considerations, and that toxics use reduction be examined as the preferred manner for coming into compliance. Authorize state agencies to require toxics use reduction plans from noncompliers.

- Mandate that state agencies coordinate their permitting activities to be multimedia to the extent possible with a focus on toxics use reduction as the preferred manner of complying.
- Provide for new regulations to be formulated and existing regulations to be changed so toxics use reduction obstacles are minimized, for innovation waivers that preserve public health and environmental protection, and for all regulatory data collection to be coordinated on a consistent facility basis.

## Implementation Actions

Two actions need to be taken to adequately address the problem of the production and use of toxic chemicals. The first is full disclosure or community "right to know" about the nature and amount of chemicals present locally. The second is that all pollution control legislation should include a toxic use reduction requirement including the following elements:

1. Empower and require agencies to phase out or ban the use of particularly problematic chemicals.
2. Require toxics users to report on the amounts of toxics that they use and that they generate as byproducts, for their facilities as a whole and for each of their production processes.
3. Require toxics users to establish plans and goals for toxics use reductions, for their facilities and for each of their production processes.
4. Empower and require agencies to set minimum toxics use reduction performance standards, which will force laggard companies to act.
5. Reform agency operations and regulations to give priority to toxics use reduction as a means of complying with laws.
6. Give community residents and workers access to information and involve them in planning processes, so that they can play a role in promoting and deciding how toxics use reduction will be accomplished. (Sugarman, March 1991, pp. 22-23)

In addition, in laws, such as the Clean Water Act and RCRA, pollution control mechanisms to stop releases should continue to be strengthened and enforcement should be stepped up. Such actions will provide additional environmental protection and keep indirect pressure on companies to undertake toxics use reduction.

*Attachment 7*

### YOU ARE A LARGE USER IF...

- your company was required to submit a Toxics Release Inventory (TRI) report to EPA

**Or if you meet all three of the following criteria**
- you are a manufacturer with a SIC code of 20 to 39
- you have 10 or more full-time employees
- you manufacture, process, or import 25,000 pounds or more of listed chemicals in one year *or* use 10,000 pounds or more of any listed chemical in one year without incorporating it into a product

### YOU ARE A LARGE QUANTITY GENERATOR IF...

**In one calendar month you...**
- generate 2,200 pounds or more of hazardous waste *or*
- generate 2,200 pounds or more of spill cleanup debris containing hazardous waste *or*
- generate more than 2.2 pounds of acutely hazardous waste *or*
- generate more than 220 pounds of spill cleanup debris containing an acutely hazardous waste *or*

**At any time you...**
- accumulate more than 2.2 pounds of acutely hazardous waste on-site

### YOU ARE A SMALL QUANTITY GENERATOR IF...

**In one calendar month you...**
- generate more than 220 pounds and less than 2,200 pounds of hazardous wastes *or*
- generate more than 220 pounds and less than 2,200 pounds of spill cleanup debris containing hazardous wastes *or*

**At any time you...**
- accumulate more than 2,200 pounds of hazardous waste on-site

### YOU ARE A CONDITIONALLY EXEMPT SMALL QUANTITY GENERATOR IF...

**In one calendar month you...**
- generate 2.2 pounds or less of acutely hazardous wastes *or*
- generate 220 pounds or less of hazardous wastes *or*
- generate 220 pounds or less of spill cleanup debris containing hazardous waste *or*

**At any time you...**
- accumulate up to 2,200 pounds of hazardous waste on-site

*Attachment 8*

## INFORMATION CLEARINGHOUSE

The Oregon Department of Environmental Quality's Waste Reduction Assistance Program offers various fact sheets, brochures and guidance materials through its Information Clearinghouse.

*Please check the box next to the information you wish to receive. If you would like more than one copy, write the number in the left margin next to the box.*

Your questions and comments are welcome. Contact the DEQ Waste Reduction Assistance Program, Attn: Joyce Thomas, 811 S.W. Sixth Avenue, Portland, Oregon 97204. Phone (503) 229-5913, or dial DEQ toll-free (within Oregon), 1-800-452-4011.

### HAZARDOUS WASTE GENERATORS
- ☐ g5  Oregon's Handbook for Small Quantity Generators of Hazardous Waste, 1992
- ☐ m6  Oregon's Handbook for Conditionally Exempt Small Quantity Generators (CEGs) of Hazardous Waste, 1992
- ☐ m4  Hazardous Waste Notification Form, 1991
- ☐ m7  Hazardous Waste Reporting Form, 1991
- ☐ m5  Standard Industrial Codes for Businesses That Generate Hazardous Waste
- ☐ f20  Hazardous Waste Fact Sheet on Counting Your Waste, 1992

### GENERAL INFORMATION: TOXICS AND HAZARDOUS WASTE
- ☐ m3  Phone List for Hazardous Waste Questions
- ☐ g11  Hazardous & Solid Waste Resource Directory, 1991
- ☐ g4  Benefitting from Toxic Substance and Hazardous Waste Reduction: A Planning Guide for Oregon Business, 1990
- ☐ m8  Toxics Use Reduction and Hazardous Waste Reduction Progress Report, 1992
- ☐ f3  State of Oregon Capacity Assurance Plan, Update, Feb. 1990

### STATUTES AND REGULATIONS
- ☐ s1  ORS 465, Reduction of Use of Toxic Substances and Hazardous Waste Generation, 1989
- ☐ s2  ORS 466, Storage, Treatment and Disposal of Hazardous Waste and PCBs, 1989
- ☐ s3  ORS 468, Pollution Control, 1989
- ☐ r1  Division 100 Hazardous Waste Management, June 1992
- ☐ r2  Toxics Use Reduction and Hazardous Waste Reduction Regulations, 1990

### METAL FINISHING, ELECTROPLATING & ELECTRONICS INDUSTRIES
- ☐ g2  Guidelines for Waste Reduction and Recycling: Metal Finishing, Electroplating, Printed Circuit Board Manufacturing, 1990

### PHOTOFINISHING INDUSTRY
- ☐ g8  Waste Reduction Guidebook for the Photofinishing Industry, 1990

# *Notes*

1. See Rubenfeld (1978, pp. 240-271).
2. See Mills (1975).
3. See Pigou (1932, pp. 159-161) and Kneese (1962).
4. A further advantage of this proposal is that, if it were fully implemented, communities, neighborhoods, or even individuals with especially high demands for environmental quality could satisfy this preference through the purchase of permits.
5. See Arthur Anderson and Company (1979).
6. Portions of this chapter are based on arguments addressed in Thompson and Jones (1982).
7. See Implications of Environmental Regulations for Energy Production and Consumption (1977, pp. 115-116).
8. See Implications of Environmental Regulations for Energy Production and Consumption (1977, pp. 115-116).
9. See McKenzie and Tullock (1978, pp. 340-357) and Buchanan (1971).
10. See Peltzman (1974), Schwartzman (1975), Wardell and Lasagna (1975) and Helms (1975).
11. On the logic of "punitive sanctions," see Blumstein et al. (1978). See also Diver (1980, pp. 257-299).
12. See Connecticut Enforcement Project (1975). See also Drayton (1980, pp. 1-40).
13. The public may be particularly cautious about nuclear hazards because government has frequently misrepresented or lied to them about the real risks. For example, the AEC insisted for years that above-ground nuclear testing was "safe." And for many years denied epidemiological evidence showing that it was not.
14. See Background Manual on the Passive Restraint Issue (1977), Air Bag and Safety Belt Fact Sheets (1977) and Sub-committee on Consumer Protection and Finance, House of representatives, Installation of Passive Restraints in Automobiles, 95th Congress, 1st Session, September 9,12, 1977.

15.   See "Gallup Poll: Public Approves of Airbags," Status Report (1977); "MVMA Poll: Air Bags 'Least Objectionable'," Status Report, (1976); and Roper Public Opinion Research Center Poll (1977).

16.   See Karr (1976) On the other hand, fewer than half of 1 percent of all new car buyers chose to buy air bags at the time of this study. This has changed remarkably since the late 1980s.

# References

Abram, D. (1988). "Merleau-Ponty and the Voice of the Earth." *Environmental Ethics,* 10, 101-120

Anderson, A. (1979). *Cost of Government Regulation Study.* New York: The Business Roundtable.

Anderson, F.J. (1991). *Natural Resources in Canada, 2nd ed. Toronto: Nelson.*

Anderson, W. T. *(1987). To Govern Evolution: Further Adventures of the Political Animal.* San Diego: Harcourt Brace Jovanovich.

Anglemeyer, M. and E. R. Seagraves. (1984). *The Natural Environment: An Annotated Bibliography of Attitudes and Values.* Washington: Smithsonian Institution Press.

Anonymous. (1989). *A History of Forest Tenure Policy,* Vol. 3. Vancouver: Forest Resources Commission Background Papers.

Anonymous. (1990). *Management Performance on Forest Tenures Study,* Vol. 3. Vancouver: Forest Resources Commission Background Papers.

Arnold, R. (1982). *At the Eye of the Storm: James Watt and the Environmentalists.* Chicago: Regnery Gateway.

Arnold, R. (1987). *Ecology Wars: Environmentalism as if People Mattered Bellevue,* Washington, DC :Free Enterprise Press.

Arrow, K.J. and R.C. Lind. (1970). "Uncertainty and the Evaluation of Public Investment Desicion." *American Economic Review,* 60 (3): 364-378.

Atkinson, S.E. and D.H. Lewis. (1974). "A Cost-Effectiveness Analysis of Alternative Air Quality Control Strategies." *Journal of Environmental Economics Management,* 1(3): 237-250.

Attfield, R. (1983). *The Ethics of Environmental Concern.* New York: Columbia University Press.

Bahro, R. (1986a). *Building the Green Movement.* Philadelphia: New Society Publishers.

Bahro, R. (1986b). *The Logic of Deliverance: On the Foundations of an Ecological Politics.* London: Schumacher Society Lecture.

Baldwin, J. H. (1985). *Environment Planning and Management.* Boulder, CO: Westview Press.

161

**162** / *References*

Balfour, L. E. (1944). *The Living Soil*. London: McMillian.

Bass, S. P. and P. Shiller. (1990). *Survey Report on Corporate Environmental Policies*. Washington, DC: Environmental Law Institute.

Beckmann, P. (1973). *Eco-Hysterics and the Technophobes*. Boulder, CO: Golem Press.

Bennett, J.T. and T.J. Di Lorenzo. (1985). *Destroying Democracy*. Washington: Cato Institute.

Bergon, F. (ed.). (1980). *The Wilderness Reader*. New York: New American Library.

Buchanan, J.M. (1971). *The Basis for Collective Action*. Morristown, NJ: General Learning Corporation.

Business International. (1990). "Managing the Environment." *The Environmental Audit, 95-107*

Cairns, J. Jr. (ed.). (1981). *The Recovery Process of Damaged Ecosystems*. Ann Arbor, MI: Ann Arbor Science.

Callicot, J. B. (1989). *In Defense of the Land Ethic: Essays on Environmental Philosophy*. Albany, NY: State University of New York Press.

Canadian Manufacturers Association. (1990). *Sustainable Development*. Ottawa: CMA.

Canan, P. and G. W. Pring. (1985). "Strategic Lawsuits Against Public Participation." *Social Problems*, 35.

Caplan, R. and The Staff of Environmental Action. (1990). *Our Earth, Ourselves*. New York: Bantam Books.

Capra, F. and C. Spretnak. (1984). *Green Politics: The Global Promise*. New York: Dutton.

Carmody, J. (1983). *Ecology and Religion: Toward a New Christian Theology of Nature*. New York: Paulist Press.

Carson, P. and J. Moulden. (1991). *Green Is Gold: Business Talking to Business About the Environmental Revolution*. Toronto: Harper Business.

Carson, R. (1961). *The Sea Around Us*. New York: New American Library.

Chapman, D. (1974). "Internalizing an Externality: A Sulphur Emission Tax and the Electric Utility Industry." In *Energy: Demand, Conservation and Institutional Problems*, edited by M.S. Macrakis. Cambridge, MA: MIT Press.

Coalition for Environmentally Responsible Economics CERES. (1989). *The Valdez Principles*.

Cohen, M. J. (1983). *Prejudice Against Nature: A Guidebook for the Liberation of Self and Planet*. National Audubon Society Expedition Institute.

Cohen, M. P. (1988). *The History of the Sierra Club: 1892-1970*. San Francisco: Sierra Club Books.

Cohn, C. (1987). "Slick'ems, Christmas Trees, and Cookie Cutters: Nuclear Language and How We Learned to Pat the Bomb." *Bulletin of the Atomic Scientists*, 435, 17-24.

Collingwood, R.G. (1945). *The Idea of Nature*. Oxford: Oxford University Press.

Collison, R. (1989). "The Greening of the Boardroom." *Report on Business Magazine*, 42-67

Commoner, B. (1990). *Making Peace With the Planet*. New York: Pantheon.

Conway, T. (1990). "Taking Stock of the Traditional Regulatory Approach" In *Getting it Green*, edited by G. B. Doern. Toronto: C.D. Howe Institute.

Cornell, N., R. Noll, and B. Weingast. (1976). "Safety Regulation." Pp. 457-504 in *Setting National Priorities: The Next Ten Years*, edited by H.M. Owen and C.L. Schultze. Washington, DC: Brookings Institute.

Cotgrove, S. and A. Duff (1981). "Environmentalism, Values and Social Change." *British Journal of Sociology*, 32, 92-110

Croner, S. (1983). *An Introduction to the World Conservation Strategy*. San Francisco: Friends of the Earth.

Dahlman, C. (1979). "The Problem of Externality." *Journal of Law and Economics*, 23, 148.

Dales, J.H. (1968). "Land, Water, and Ownership." *Canadian Journal of Economics*, 1(4): 791-804.

Dales, J.H. (1968). *Pollution, Property, and Prices*. Toronto: University of Toronto Press.

Daly, H.E. and J. Cobb. (1989). *For the Common Good: Redirecting the Economy Towards Community, the Environment, and a Sustainable Future*. Boston: Beacon Press.

Davis, O.A. and M.I. Kamien. (1970). "Externalities, Information, and Alternative Collection Actions." Pp. 82-104 in *Public Expenditure and Policy Analysis*, edited by R. A. Haveman and J. Margolis. Chicago, IL: Rand McNally.

Dutt, R.B. (1988). "Environmental Monitoring and Reporting." In *UNEP Industry and Environment*, Vol.II 4. 33-38

Elkington, J. (1990). "The Environmental Audit: A Green Filter for Company Policies, Plants, Processes and Products." *World Wildlife Fund, Sustainability and World Wide Fund for Nature*. London, England

Environmental Policy Center, The. (1990). *Issues Addressed by Existing Corporate Policies on Health, Safety and the Environment: An Informal Survey*. Law Companies Environmental Group, 1828 L Street, NW, Washington, DC. 25 pp.

Ferguson, D. and N. Ferguson (1983). *Sacred Cows at the Public. Trough Bend, OR: Maverick Publications.*

*Fisher, A. and F.M. Peterson. (1978). "The Environment in Economics: A Survey." Journal of Economic Literature*, 27, 241.

Fisher, S. (1989). "Clean Green Profits: The Green Revolution." *Vista*, 35-47

Fisher, S. (1990). "Clean Green Profits." *Vista*, 2 9, 39

Fishkin, J.S. 1984. *Beyond Subjective Morality: Ethical Reasoning and Political Philosophy*. New Haven: Yale University Press.

Foreman, D. (ed.). (1986). *Ecodefense: A Field Guide to Monkeywrenching* Tucson, AZ: Ned Ludd Books.

Fox, S. (1981). *John Muir and His Legacy: The American Conservation Movement*. Boston: Little, Brown.

Frey, R.G. (1983). *Rights, Killing and Suffering*. Oxford: Oxford University Press.

Friedman, F. (1990). *Practical Guide to Environmental Management*. Washington, DC: Environmental Law Institute.

Gibson, R.B. (1990). "Out of Control and Beyond Understanding: Acid Rain as a Political Dilemma." In *Managing Leviathan: Environmental Politics and the Administrative State,* edited by R. Paehlke and D. Torgerson. Toronto: Broadview Press.

Gorden, R. (1978). "The Hobbling of Coal: Policy and Regulatory Uncertainties." *Science,* 153-158.

Gray, R. (1990). "The Accountants Task as a Friend to the Earth."

Greenpeace. 1990. "What Works: An Oral History of Five Greenpeace Campaigns." *Greenpeace: The Next Ten Years,* 151, 9-13

Greenpeace Chronicles, California Edition. (1988). "The Tide Turned: Mark Dubois and the Defense of the Stanislaus River."

Gregg, A. and M. Posner (1990). *The Big Picture.* Toronto: MacFarlane, Walter & Ross.

Gunn, A.S. (1980). "Why Should We Care About Rare Species?" *Environmental Ethics,* 21, 17-38

Griffen, J.M. (1974). "An Econometric Evaluation of Sulphur Taxes." *Journal of Political Economy,* 82(4): 669-688.

Hanson, P.P. (1986). *Environmental Ethics: Philosophical and Policy Perspectives.* Burnaby, B.C.: Institute for the Humanities.

Hardin, G. and J. Baden. (eds.). (1977). *Managing the Commons.* San Francisco: Freeman.

Hays, S.P. (1987). *Beauty, Health and Permanence: Environmental Politics in the United States, 1955-1985.* Cambridge: Cambridge University Press.

Hedstrom, G.S. and J.E. Obbagy. 1988. "Environmental Auditing: Global Perspective - Transition to the 1990's." *UNEP Industry and Environment,* 2(4): 11-13

Helms, R.B. (1975). *Drug Development and Marketing.* Washington, DC: American Enterprise Institute.

Henderson, H. (1981). *The Politics of the Solar Age: Alternatives to Economics.* New York: Anchor/Doubleday.

Heritage Forests Society. (1990). *Towards the Survival of Old-Growth Forests.* Vancouver: HFS.

Industry, Science and Technology Canada. (1991). *Competitiveness in the 90's — Environmental Performance.* BC: Canada.

International Chamber of Commerce. (1988). "ICC Position Paper on Environmental Auditing." *UNEP Industry and Environment,* 2(4). 14-17

International Chamber of Commerce. (1989). *Environmental Auditing.* Paris, France.

Jackson, S. (1990). "Screaming Green Murder." *Director,* 44(11): 56- 61

Jones, L.R. (1982). *Regulatory Policy and Practices.* New York: Praeger Scientific.

Kneese, A.V. (1962). *Water Pollution: Economic Aspects and Research Needs.* Washington, DC: Resources for the Future.

Kneese, A.V. (1975). *Pollution, Prices and Public Policy.* Washington, DC: Brookings Institution.

Lave, L.B. and E.P. Seskin. (1977). *Air Pollution and Human Health.* Baltimore, MD: Johns Hopkins Press.

Lewis-Beck, M.S. and J.R. Alford. (1980). "Can Government Regulate Safety? The Coal Mine Example." *American Political Science Review,* 74(3), 745-756.

Makower, J.,J. Elkington, and J. Hailes. (1991). *The Green Consumer Supermarket Guide*. London: Tilden Press, Penguin Books.

Maxwell, S. (1990). "The Rise of the Environmental Audit." *Accounting*, 70.

McCloskey, M. (1991). "Business, Environmentalism, and the Marketplace: New Currents and Possibilities." *Autzen Lecture Series*. Oregon Humanities Center, University of Oregon, Eugene, Oregon.

McKenzie, R.B. and G. Tullock. (1978). *Modern Political Economy*. New York: McGraw-Hill.

Mendelhoff, J. (1979). *Regulating Safety: An Economic and Political Analysis of the Occupational Health and Safety Policy*. Cambridge, MA: MIT Press.

Miller, G.T. (1990). *Living in the Environment*. Sixth Edition. Belmont, CA: Wadsworth Publishing Company,

Mills, E.S. (ed.). (1975). *Economic Analysis and Environmental Problems*. New York: Columbia University Press.

National Highway Safety Needs Report. (1976). Washington, DC: U.S. Department of Transportation.

Newcomb, R. (1978). "The American Coal Industry." *Current History*, 74(2), 206-228.

Oregon Department of Environmental Quality. (1989). "Oregon's Toxic Use Reduction and Hazardous Waste Reduction Act." *Fact Sheet*. Portland.

Oregon Department of Environmental Quality. (1990). "Information Clearinghouse." Portland.

Oregon Department of Environmental Quality. (1991). "Benefiting From Toxic Substance and Hazardous Waste Reduction." Portland.

Oregon State Public Interest Group. (1990). "Toxic Use Reduction, from Pollution to Prevention." *Fact Sheet*. Portland.

Page, T., R.H. Harris, and S.S. Epstein. (1976). "Drinking Water and Cancer Mortality in Louisiana." *Science*, 55.

Peat Marwilck Stevenson and Kellog. (1991). "Environmental Action Handbook: An Operational Guide for Business." Prepared for Industry, Science and Technology, Canada, British Columbia, Canada.

Peltzman, S. (1973). "An Evaluation of Consumer Protection Legislation: The 1962 Drug Amendments." *Journal of Political Economy*, 81, 1049-1091.

Peltzman, S. (1974). Regulation of Pharmaceutical Innovation: The 1962 Amendments. Washington, DC: American Enterprise Institute.

Pepper, D. (1985). *The Roots of Modern Environmentalism*. London:

Peskin, H.M., and E.P. Seskin. (eds.). (1975). *Cost Benefit Analysis and Air Pollution Policy*. Washington, DC: Urban Institute.

Pezzey, J. (1988). "Market Mechanisms of Pollution Control: 'Polluter Pays,' Economic and Practical Aspects." In R.K. Turner *Sustainable Environmental Management, Principles and Practice*, edited by R.K. Turner. London: Belhaven Press.

Phillips, D. (1990). "Breakthrough for Dolphins: How We Did It." *Earth Island Journal*, 26-27

Pigou, A.C. (1932). *The Economics of Welfare*. London: McMillan.

Pinchot, G. (1947). *Breaking New Ground*. New York: Harcourt, Brace and Co..

**166** / *References*

Pinchot, G. (1967). *The Fight for Conservation*. Seattle: University of Washington Press.

Plumwood, V. and R. Routley. (1982). "World Rainforest Destruction: The Social Factors." *Ecologist*, 121, 4-22

Pollution Probe. (1990). *Canadian Green Consumer Guide: How You Can Help*. Toronto: McClelland and Stewart.

Porritt, J. (1985). *Green: The Politics of Ecology Explained*. New York: Basil Blackwell.

Portnoy, P.R. (1979). "Efficient Use of Standards and Enforcement: The Case of Pollution Controls." *Policy Analysis*, 5(4): 512-524.

Postel, S. and L. Heise. (1988). *Reforesting the Earth* Worldwatch Institute: Worldwatch Paper.

Priznar, F.J. (1990). "Trends in Environmental Auditing." *Environmental Law Reporter*, 10179-10183

Ridgeway, J. (1970). *The Politics of Ecology*. New York: E.P. Dutton.

Rubenfeld, D.L. (1978). "Market Approaches to the Measurement of the Benefits of Air Pollution Abatement." Pp. 240-271 in *Approaches to Controlling Air Pollution*, edited by A. Friedlander. Cambridge, MA: MIT Press.

Ryan, W. (1991). "An Ounce of Toxic Pollution Prevention." National Environmental Law Center. Center for Policy Alternatives.

Schwartzman, D. (1975). *The Expected Return From Pharmaceutical Research*. Washington, DC: American Enterprise Institute.

Shea, C.P. (1989). "Doing Well by Doing Good." World Watch, 24.

Smith, E. et al. (1990). "The Greening of Corporate America." *Business Week*, p. 96.

Smith, R.S. (1974). "The Feasibility of an 'Injury Tax' Approach to Occupational Safety." *Journal of Law and Contemporary Problems*, 38, 730-744.

Smith, R.S. (1976). *The Occupational Safety and Health Act*. Washington, DC: American Enterprise Institute.

Snyder, J. (1991). *Report Summaries*. Portland: O'Neill and Company.

Steger, W. and J. Bowemaster. (1990). *A Citizen's Guide to Environmental Action*. New York: Byron Priess Books.

Sugarman, Q. (1991). "Toxic Truth and Consequences." Oregon State Public Interest Group, Portland.

Sustainability. (1991). "Going Green." Summary of Environmental Management Consulting Services. The People's Hall, Freston Rd.

Sutherland, F.P. and V. Parker (1988). "Environmentalists at Law" Pp. 181-190 In *Crossroads: Environmental Priorities for the Future*, edited by P. Borelli. Washington, DC: Island Press.

Swolop, S. and A. Barrett. (1990). "Business and the Environment." *Financial World*, 41-49

Tietenberg, T.H. (1973). "Specific Taxes and Pollution Control: A General Equilibrium Analysis." *Quarterly Journal of Economics*, 87(4): 503-522.

Thompson, F. and L.R. Jones. (1982). *Regulatory Policy and Practices*. New York: Praeger Scientific.

Tokar, B. (1990). "Marketing the Environment," *Z Magazine*, 15-21

Tuer, C.B. (1990). *Good Planets are Hard to Find: Prescriptions for Everyday Action*. Calgary: Bidell Publishing.

Turner, T. (1988). "The Legal Eagles." In *Crossroads: Environmental Priorities for the Future*, edited by P. Borelli. Washington, DC: Island Press.

Tusa, W. (1990). "Developing an Environmental Program." *Risk Management*, 24-29.

Tversky, A. and D. Kahneman. (1974). "Judgement Under Uncertainty: Heuristics and Biases." *Science*, 1124-1131.

United Nations Environment Programme. (1988). "Environmental Auditing." *Industry and Environment*, 4, 2

United Nations Environment Program. (1990). "Environmental Auditing." Industry and Environment Workshop, Technical Report Series No. 2, Paris, France.

U.S. Regulatory Council. (1980). *Regulating with Common Sense: A Progress Report on Innovative Regulatory Techniques*. Washington, DC: Author.

Van Den Bosch, R. (1983). *The Pesticide Conspiracy*. Garden City, NY: Doubleday.

Wardell, W.M. and L. Lasagna. (1975). *Regulation and Drug Development*. Washington, DC: American Enterprise Institute.

Warwick, F. (1984). "Deep Ecology: A New Philosophy of our Time?" *The Ecologist*, 145(6): 194-200

Washington Post, The. (1991). "Spill Sparks Corporate Ethics Code." The Eugene Register Guard.

Watson, D. (1990). "Green With Anger" *Vancouver Magazine*, May, pp. 39-50, 68, 100-103, 113

Watson, P. and W. Rogers. (1982). *Sea Shepherd: My Fight for Whales and Seals*. New York, W.W. Norton.

Weiner, J. (1990). *The Next 100 Years: Shaping the Fate of Our Earth*. New York: Bantam Books.

Weston, J. (ed.). (1986). *Red and Green, The New Politics of the Environment*. London

Whelan, E. (1985). *Toxic Terror*. Ottawa, IL: Jameson Books.